IMPERFECT
lives

scrapbooking the reality
▸ *of your everyday*

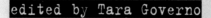
edited by Tara Governo

Memory Makers Books
Cincinnati, Ohio
www.memorymakersmagazine.com

Published by Memory Makers Books, an imprint of F+W Publications, Inc., 4700 East Galbraith Road, Cincinnati, Ohio 45236. (800) 289-0963. First edition.

10 09 08 07 06 5 4 3 2 1

Distributed in Canada by Fraser Direct
100 Armstrong Avenue
Georgetown, ON, Canada L7G 5S4
Tel: (905) 877-4411

Distributed in the U.K. and Europe by David & Charles
Brunel House, Newton Abbot, Devon, TQ12 4PU, England
Tel: (+44) 1626 323200, Fax: (+44) 1626 323319
Email: postmaster@davidandcharles.co.uk

Distributed in Australia by Capricorn Link
P.O. Box 704, S. Windsor, NSW 2756 Australia
Tel: (02) 4577-3555

Editor: Christine Doyle
Designer: Lisa Buchanan-Kuhn, www.curiopress.com
Production Coordinator: Matt Wagner
Photographer: Jim Gilmore, OMS

Library of Congress Cataloging-in-Publication Data

Imperfect lives : scrapbooking the reality of your everyday / edited by
Tara Governo. -- 1st ed.
     p. cm.
   Includes index.
   ISBN-10: 1-892127-94-6 (alk. paper)
   ISBN-13: 978-1-892127-94-5 (alk. paper)
   1. Photograph albums. 2. Scrapbooks. I. Governo, Tara. II. Memory
Makers Books.
   TR501.I47 2006
   746.593--dc22
                        2006020418

ABOUT THE AUTHOR

Tara Governo is an avid scrapbooker and loves the idea of preserving memories—all memories of the journey of life. It isn't just about the crowning moments; it is about the entire range of experiences. Tara's vision for *Imperfect Lives* was to create the means for others to tell the stories of life that often go untold.

DEDICATION

To my husband Darrin…

You are my soul mate, my biggest cheerleader and fan, my life mentor and my best friend. Thank you for believing in me, for encouraging me and for loving me enough to sacrifice yourself. I love you.

To my beautiful sons Cole and Nate…

I love you both with all of my heart! Thank you for showing me a how to love a life I never could have imagined. You are my gifts from God.

To my older sister Meghan…

I can't imagine life without you…you have been there for me from the first day of my life. You are my best friend and confidant… words cannot express my love for you.

To my mother…

Thank you for teaching me to be a strong and independent woman, a self-starter, a thinker, a planner, a dreamer, to be myself and to speak my mind. And most importantly, thank you for giving me the gift of life.

To my friend Dawn…

Thank you for introducing me to such an amazing hobby…for being my teacher, my mentor, my coach, my cheerleader and, most importantly, my friend.

To my friend Jennie…

Thank you so much for being there for me and for your unwavering friendship and support. I appreciate you more than you will ever know.

ACKNOWLEDGMENTS

I would like to thank Tricia Waddell and Christine Doyle for believing in this project and F+W Publications, Inc. for supporting the concept of *Imperfect Lives*. I would also like to express my gratitude to all of the artists in the book who were willing to share each personal and artistic piece of their lives.

TABLE OF CONTENTS

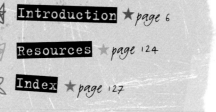

would you want to know? ???

THE CRYSTAL BALL

UNLOCK THE mystery OF LIFE

SUCCESS—FAILURE

IN AN INSTANT, I COULD SEE,
WHAT THE FUTURE HOLDS FOR ME.
DO I WANT TO KNOW WHAT THE FUTURE HOLDS,
OR LIVE MY LIFE AS EACH DAY UNFOLDS.

> "THERE IS NO AGONY LIKE
> BEARING AN UNTOLD
> STORY INSIDE OF YOU."
> MAYA ANGELOU

INTRODUCTION >>>

"Would anyone looking at your scrapbooks think your life was perfect?" This was a question someone asked on one of my favorite message boards just a few short months after I started this journey. Who knew where this would go? It could have just stalled as many other ideas or projects before this...or would this be bigger than me and take on a life of its own? It did, and *Imperfect Lives* was born.

My life is not perfect, not even close. My childhood was not the happiest, my adult years have been rocky to say the least, my relationships are not perfect, not one of them. Even my relationship with my wonderful and supportive husband is flawed, just a little... sorry Darrin! My children are not perfect. As much as I would like them to be, they are not. But I love them and can't live without them.

Life is full of ups and downs, and no one is immune to the roller coaster of life. Can you appreciate the good without the bad? I don't think so. The bad stuff makes us who we are, it builds character and strength, it teaches us life lessons, and it makes us appreciate the good stuff. Most importantly, it reminds us to nurture and value the people and the things we love and cherish the most.

In the pages to follow, you will see honest, real, edgy, quirky, humorous layouts that tell the "real" story of life. You will laugh out loud, you will cry, you will get goose bumps (you know, the good kind). To all of the brilliant women that shared your personal stories, thank you from the bottom of my heart. To those of you reading this, welcome to our Imperfect Lives.

THE CRYSTAL BALL

The Story Behind the Layout

SUPPLIES:
Patterned papers (7 gypsies, K&Company); chipboard letters, acrylic flower accent (Heidi Swapp); rub-on letters, words, phrases (Autumn Leaves, Bobarbo, Making Memories, My Mind's Eye); brad (American Crafts); cardstock; acrylic paint; stamping ink; pen; staples

Would you want to know? Would you change the path of your life if you could? Or would it just create an altered reality with different situations and a new set of challenges? Would it take away from the experience of life, and the mystery of what lies ahead? I often tell myself, "If I only knew..." Sometimes I wish I could see a glimpse of my future...but do I really want to know? Absolutely not! I would prefer to live each day without knowing what lies ahead. Seeing your future is like watching the ending of a movie first. Life is not about the destination...the reward is in the journey.

TARA GOVERNO

★ Gilbert, Arizona

CaRefREE

SWEET !6

F irst love (first heartache)

M y own personal chef (mom cooks great)

P erfect figure (can eat anything)

N o money problems (no bills to pay)

N o worries (only what to wear)

H anging out with friends (so much fun)

THROUGH THE
EYES OF A CHILD >

"THERE IS ALWAYS ONE MOMENT IN CHILDHOOD WHEN THE DOOR OPENS AND LETS THE FUTURE IN."
DEEPAK CHOPRA

The memories of childhood are vivid, but like a dream…no beginning, no end…just flashes of time stored in our mind. Anything can trigger these memories: a photograph, a word, a song, a smell. These memories never leave, never fade…they are burned into our mind, our soul. In a flash, something small will trigger one of these memories and we quickly revert back…just for a second. The feeling is overwhelming, like you are there, like it happened yesterday, but just for a moment. Then we are back to reality as quickly as we left.

Childhood is a time of innocence and of inexperience. It is the beginning of life. It is a time of growth, for your body, your mind, your soul. The memories of childhood last a lifetime. Life starts here.

CAREFREE AT
SWEET 16

JOURNALING

First love (first heartache)
No worries (only what to wear)
My own personal chef (mom cooks great)
No money problems (no bills to pay)
Perfect figure (can eat anything)
Acting silly (no one cares)
Hanging out with friends (so much fun)

CORINNE DELIS

★ The Netherlands

SUPPLIES:
Patterned papers (Autumn Leaves, Chatterbox); textured cardstock (Bazzill); letter stickers (American Crafts, BasicGrey, Doodlebug Design, Flair Designs, KI Memories, Pebbles, Wordsworth); chipboard letters (BasicGrey); chalk ink (Clearsnap); acrylic paint; pens; staples

The Story Behind the Layout

I can remember how I was back then and how carefree I felt at sixteen—I could handle the whole world.

When I am in the midst of diaper changing, breaking my neck over 600 dinky toys, starting to diet again and having sleepless nights about bills to pay, I wish I was sixteen again, just for one moment.

and I think to myself, what a

WONDERFUL WORLD

WONDERFUL WORLD

SUPPLIES:
Patterned papers (My Mind's Eye, Paper Loft); textured cardstock (Bazzill); rub-on flowers (KI Memories, My Mind's Eye); ribbon (Michaels); chalk ink (Clearsnap); large and mini brads (Making Memories); letter stickers (Paper Loft); label maker (DYMO)

The Story Behind the Layout

One day this past autumn, I took my boys to the park so they could run off some energy. I was sitting on the bench thinking of all the things I needed to do, and worrying about how much time we were spending at the park, when I looked up and saw them throwing leaves around. It made me realize that sometimes we need to stop what we're doing and actually take a look around, because the world around us is so beautiful. Sometimes we forget to enjoy the little things. My boys are growing up so very fast, spending moments like this with them should be my priority. It's amazing what you can learn from children!

ERIN KEENER

★ Albuquerque, New Mexico

I am a married mother of two living in New Mexico. I started scrapbooking after my second son was born, and it quickly escalated into a full on passion of mine. Scrapbooking is my creative outlet. It's my "me" time. Not only am I documenting special moments so my boys can look back on them and remember things they otherwise may not, but I'm creating art! I've learned so much from those around me about how to capture precious moments, and I've found that sometimes the most special pictures are those that are unplanned and candid. I absorb creativity from the scrapbookers I've met from around the world, and love that I belong to such a special community of amazing women! I feel so passionate about scrapbooking that I would like to design my own line of products. Scrapbooking has opened many new doors to me, not only in the great friends I've made along the way, but also in some fabulous opportunities.

Lick-finger-rub

easter 1979

i miss your cleaning the "kid" off my face.

i see this and my skin CRAWLS... all i can remember is my mom's spit-laden finger leering at me, coming in close for the oh-so-tortureous face "cleaning". eeew! but then i look closer. and suddenly i see her heart on my sleeve. literally. she worked for weeks to make all us "girls" matching outfits for easter sunday. and suddenly, i wish i were there right now.

LICK-FINGER-RUB

SUPPLIES:
Patterned papers (Autumn Leaves); textured cardstock (Bazzill); rub-on letters and elements (Autumn Leaves, FontWerks); photo corners; lace trim; pen

JOURNALING

I see this and my skin crawls...all I can remember is my mom's spit-laden finger leering at me, coming in close for the oh-so-torturous face "cleaning." Eeew! But, then I look closer. And suddenly I see her heart on my sleeve. Literally. She worked for three weeks to make all us "girls" matching outfits for Easter Sunday. And suddenly, I wish I were there right now.

The Story Behind the Layout

Late one night, after a long day of being "mommy" to my three kids, I came across this old photo of my mom, sister and me on an Easter morning. So many memories came flooding back. I vividly remembered her making matching Easter dresses for us all, the horrid "fitting sessions" we endured while getting "poked" with straight pins, and the way she would lick her fingers and wipe the smudges off of our faces. It always grossed me out as a kid, but now as a mom myself, I realize I've resorted to the same tactics myself. It is ironic how diligently we strive to not be like our mothers, but in that moment, I knew there was no one else I'd rather be more like.

TIA BENNETT

★ Puyallup, Washington

I am thirty years old, a wife of eleven years to a very patient man, mom to three very heroic children, and an optimist by choice! I am the girl who, in first grade, laid her head down and cried when her teacher told her she had to color inside the lines. It wasn't a matter of skill—I was pretty accomplished at being precise—I just wanted to add some "scenery" is all! To this day, I continue my drive to challenge the ordinary, and to color outside the lines, with a creative energy that lives within my every breath.

My funky, artistic style made the evolution to paper crafting in late 2004, though I have been involved in some form of art my whole life. In that short time, I have managed to be published in many scrapbook and paper crafting magazines. I also have been fortunate enough to design rubber stamps and fonts and to participate on design teams for manufacturers.

happy

❀ *childhood memories* ❀

............toddler

❀ family

My grandma's KitcHeN

105th Pl.
Chicago, IL

June 1964

little Dawny

almost 2 years old

so happy...so loved

MY GRANDMA'S KITCHEN

SUPPLIES:
Patterned paper (Lasting Impressions, Melissa Frances, me & my BIG Ideas, Art Warehouse); flowers and floral stamp (Making Memories); alphabet stickers (Doodlebug); rub-ons (Autumn Leaves, Karen Foster, Doodlebug); tags (Rusty Pickle); brads (Bazzill); jewels (Heidi Swapp); rick rack (Wrights); ribbon (Offray, Making Memories, May Arts); buttons; lace; ring; safety pin; sewing machine; acrylic paint

The Story Behind the Layout

When I see this photo of me in my grandmother's kitchen, I'm transported to a time and place I can barely remember. I somehow recall the smells and the warmth of the kitchen, the sunlight through the window, and my grandma's loving voice. It brings back memories of the things we did there together, in her house, and how much I loved to be with her.

Today I find myself, a couple of generations later, producing those same pictures for my daughter. As time passes in her life, she too may pull out Mom's photos and be transported to a nice warm kitchen on a sunny day, and feel that same lost innocence where all is good. Hopefully she will remember my loving voice and fully understand just how much I loved her.

DAWN TARANTO

★ Gilbert, Arizona

I'm married to Bob, my husband of twenty-four years. After twenty years of marriage, and without ever having seriously considered children, we decided, very unexpectedly, that we really wanted a child of our own. It consumed us! It came on so suddenly that I'm still reeling. Gratefully, though, we were blessed with a beautiful little girl we named Kailee. She's now three years old and, with the exception of some sleepless nights, and sacrificed freedom, and additional cost, and not always being able to just get up and go, and not having the freedom to live where we want—oops, I seem to have gotten sidetracked... sorry!—we LOVE her to pieces. I've never felt the kind of deep down joy and happiness that she's provided!

little Dawny

almost 2 years old

so happy...so loved

younger

OHIO

Note to ↑ self:

Don't be in such a hurry to grow up. You will be an adult much longer than you will be a child. You are smarter than you think you are, so don't sell yourself short. Listen more and talk less. You will learn more from others if you keep your mouth shut. Learn from your mistakes. It isn't a mistake if you learn the lesson. You will find prince charming sooner than you think. Learn how to say "no" to other people. If you don't, others will take advantage of your kindness. Embrace who you are and appreciate the gifts you have to offer.

With love,
▼ ▼ ▼ ▼ ▼ ▼ ▼ ▼
The older, wiser Tara
XOXO

unique

creative

strong

5 TIME

NOTE TO (YOUNGER) SELF

SUPPLIES:
Patterned paper (7 gypsies); textured cardstock (Bazzill); corrugated cardboard (Paper Company); chipboard letters, acrylic flowers (Heidi Swapp); chipboard flower (Everlasting Keepsakes); metal word accents (KI Memories); rub-on elements (7 gypsies, Autumn Leaves, Making Memories, My Mind's Eye); stamping ink; acrylic paint; pen; envelope

JOURNALING

Note to self:

Don't be in such a hurry to grow up. You will be an adult much longer than you will be a child. You are smarter than you think you are, so don't sell yourself short. Listen more and talk less. You will learn more from others if you keep your mouth shut. Learn from your mistakes. It isn't a mistake if you learn the lesson. You will find prince charming sooner than you think. Learn how to say "no" to other people. If you don't, others will take advantage of your kindness. Embrace who you are and the gifts you have to offer.

With love,

The older, wiser Tara

XOXO

The Story Behind the Layout

When I look at childhood photographs of myself, I often wish I knew then what I know now as an adult. I sometimes wish for the opportunity to speak to my younger self. I want to tell her that she will make it through the hard times, she is strong, and she will endure the many challenges she will face growing up. I wrote the letter in hopes to heal the wounds of my past and to encourage that little girl to be the best she can be. The whole process of writing the letter was healing and empowering. I wrote all of the things I needed to hear growing up and used this experience as a way to remember to tell my own children the things they want and need to hear as well.

TARA GOVERNO

★ Gilbert, Arizona

I discovered scrapbooking in March of 2005 and instantly became obsessed and addicted to this amazing hobby. I enjoy being creative and make a little time each day to work on creative projects. I love the idea of leaving behind a piece of myself through the art of scrapbooking, and I enjoy telling the stories of my life, and the lives of my children, for future generations to enjoy.

DO'IN MY DADDY'S TIME

No 4 year old child should schedule their life around visiting day at the jail.

No 4 year old child should know that an ankle bracelet isn't a form of jewelry.

1-4

No 4 year old child should ask "whose house am I sleeping at today?"

No 4 year old child should greet other kids in the park by saying, Hi, my name is .... and my daddy's in jail.

No 4 year old child .... street.

No 4 year old shoul .... sound like handcuffs.

.... living down the

Your life has been a series of traumas and disappointments and I don't have an abundance of hope that it will change in the near future. For the past 4 years, you have been doing someone else's time in your very personal way. Your father's battle with alcohol and drug addiction has changed who you are, forever. Children with an incarcerated parent express a broad range of emotions, including fear, anxiety, anger, sadness, loneliness and guilt. You have a huge fear of abandonment and with all that has happened in your short life, I am sure that will always be an issue for you. I have struggled through the years on how much of the truth to tell you and then decided it was better not to hide anything and be very honest without shaming you in the process. Anger, has been your constant companion, as you work through your disappointment, resentments, frustration and sense of loss. As you get older, I am sure you will feel responsible for your mom and dad's behaviors and suffer the guilt that all children feel of not being "enough" to motivate your parents into changing their lives or overcoming their addictions. All children of addicts feel this way, but when you are older and understand the illness of addiction, you will see how cunning, baffling and powerful and even stronger than a parents love, these addictions can be. I pray every day that you will take a totally different path in life and learn from all the examples of destruction around you. 7 out of 10 children with an incarcerated parent will one day themselves end up in prison, but life is all about choices, and it is up to you alone to choose what you want to do with your life. Until my last breath and beyond, I am here for you, Alexis, to show you the love and security that was your birthright.

Grandma Robbin

LIFE TIME

No 4 year old child should have post traumatic stress syndrome.

0002003

DOIN' MY DADDY'S TIME

SUPPLIES:
Patterned paper (KI Memories); textured cardstock (Bazzill); clock embellishment (Rusty Pickle); letter stickers (Sticker Studio); brad (Making Memories); watch and clock parts

JOURNALING

No 4 year old child should schedule their life around visiting day at the jail. No 4 year old child should go into hysteria at the sound of jangling keys, because they sound like handcuffs. No 4 year old child should wet herself, because she sees a police car driving down the street. No 4 year old child should ask "whose house am I sleeping at today?" No 4 year old child should know that an ankle bracelet isn't a form of jewelry. No 4 year old child should greet other kids in the park by saying, Hi, my name is... and my daddy's in jail. No 4 year old child should have post traumatic stress syndrome. BUT YOU DO... Because you are doing your daddy's time

The Story Behind the Layout

I took these photos of my granddaughter with this layout in mind. I had been thinking about how the absence of her mother and her father's repeated incarcerations had affected her life. The summer that these photos were taken, her father had been arrested several times while in her company. The repeated arrests have had a very traumatic effect on her, changing her forever. I started doing research on how children are affected by having an imprisoned parent. I was already seeing the undeniable strain and the signs of post traumatic stress syndrome in her. I decided to use these very powerful photos and complete this layout to give a voice to what she has been through, and to let her know that she is not alone. This layout, and some other reality layouts, will be part of an album called the "Book of Truths" that I will give to Alexis when she is grown. Families tend to keep a lot of secrets about unpleasant events. The problem with this is that it doesn't validate what a person has been through and leaves them with a lot of unresolved conflicts. When there is a big difference between childhood memories and the stories a family tells, you end up with an adult who doesn't trust her own instincts or her own reality.

ROBBIN WOOD

★ Spokane, Washington

I am a grandmother who has raised my five-year-old granddaughter, Alexis, since she was about six months old. I retired from the corporate world seven years ago due to liver failure and a severe back injury. I thought my life was over, but my Higher Power had something different in mind for me. Through a series of life changing events, which at the time I thought were devastating, he put me in a position where I could raise Alexis. It was divine intervention at work. I am passionate about scrapbooking for many reasons. Life has dealt my granddaughter a very difficult hand. I want her to be able to see in a visual form that she is very loved and valued. It is something money cannot buy, a permanent gift from the heart. I was a crafter with my own small business for the past thirty years, before I started scrapbooking. I love how all the other crafts that I have done in the past can be incorporated into my scrapbooking today. It never bores me; there is something always new and fresh to try.

Your mother was seven months pregnant when she found out that you were on the way. She was not happy at all, she never wanted another baby. Till this day, you always have this feeling deep inside of not being wanted or that you should never ever have been born. Your childhood was far from perfect with a dominant mother that ruled the house and the minds of her children. At that time it seemed normal to you. You were forced to work at the age of only fifteen. It was either that or you could move out of the house. You always wanted to be a designer and have an education in that direction, but that was out of the question. So you started paving the streets just like your father and grandfather did.

When we met it was like we found our soul mates. By bringing you into my family, you noticed rapidly that things went very different in other peoples homes than it did in yours. The childhood you had turned out to be one big façade and things happened so fast that you could not deal with this emotionally. You built up this wall around your feelings and decided, after so many problems, not to have any contact anymore with your mother and your sister.

Today we are 8,5 years further since the day we met and you are really trying to find the real you (since that you thought you were was created to please everyone else). You have changed on this road from a very sensitive boy into a hard and cynical man, desperately trying to bring back a part of that sweet boy within you. It is a long and hard road, but you know you're half way there and I know together we can make this. **We shall find You.**

FINDING YOU

SUPPLIES:
Patterned papers (7 gypsies, KI Memories, Provo Craft); textured cardstock (Bazzill); foam alphabet stamps (Heidi Swapp, Li'l Davis Designs, Making Memories); chalk ink (Clearsnap); pen

The Story Behind the Layout

For the last few years, my husband has searched on a daily basis to find himself. His search has had a significant influence on me and the rest of our family. With all the highs and lows, it feels like we are on a roller coaster. But with each passing year, it seems the downs are not as deep as they once were, and I feel positive changes coming from this experience. It has been so rewarding to watch him change into a person who is more secure and dares to say "no." It has been hard times for him and for us as a couple, but seeing him grow has been worth the struggle. By creating this layout I also want him to know how proud I am for coming this far already.

CORINNE DELIS

★ The Netherlands

I am thirty-one years old and married to my husband, Raymond. I am a mother of two beautiful sons, Anthony and Jadenn. I have a degree in designing and live happily in the Netherlands. I have always loved to draw, paint, journal and take photographs. Scrapbooking is my passion; it allows me to combine all of my hobbies! I started scrapbooking in 2004, and my life has changed 180 degrees. I can't even begin to explain, but it has brought joy to my soul. My goal for the future is to design my own book or paper line.

YOU'LL HAVE TO TAKE...

SUPPLIES:
Patterned paper (Junkitz); textured cardstock (Bazzill); rub-on textures (My Mind's Eye); chipboard letters (Heidi Swapp); gel pen (American Crafts); stamping ink

The Story Behind the Layout

I love to take pictures of my children, and Jamie is my most willing participant. She loves to pose! Unfortunately, even as a pre-teen, she is already having skin problems. Thankfully, I've learned the value of photo editing software. But it occurred to me that when she was grown, she might look back at my scrapbooks and think that her skin (and our lives) were always flawless. I think it's important to document the rough times along with the birthdays, trips to the zoo and family gatherings. So it was time to put some of those blemishes back into the picture. Jamie loves any scrapbook page about her, and though she initially balked at the highlighting of her imperfections, she eventually decided this page was perfect for this publication.

CHRISTY O'BRYANT

★ Justin, Texas

I am a pediatric physical therapist currently working in home health care. Because of this job, I drive all over and work in the homes of children with various developmental delays. I'm married to a wonderful man who supports my goals and dreams. We have three beautiful children: Jamie, Hunter and Hannah (twins!). I started scrapbooking about three and a half years ago when a scrapbook store opened down the street from me. Having always been a crafter, I had to check it out. I was instantly mesmerized by all of the "stuff" and have been hooked ever since.

CON*ESSO*S of a TE*EN WAITRESS*

I have a confession to make...
The five years I was a waitress at
Rockwell's were some of the best years of my life.

Yes, my feet killed me after hours on the job,
Yes, I became attached to my 'regulars',
Yes, I missed all the fun everyone else had in high school,
No, I never got to go to a football or basketball game on
a Friday night cause I needed the money,
Yes, I even liked the nasty customers and
No, I never spit in their food,
Yes, the customer is always right!
Yes, I am a very good tipper now and almost always leave 20%,
Yes, I would do it again in a heartbeat if I needed to.

Prime Rib
-medium
chicken
parm w/
rice
diet + H2O

CONFESSIONS OF A TEEN

SUPPLIES:
Patterned papers (Imagination Project, KI Memories); textured cardstock (Bazzill); letter stickers (Chatterbox, Making Memories); ribbons (Doodlebug Design, May Arts); clips, clipboard (Provo Craft); die-cut accents (KI Memories); crystal flower accent (source unknown); pen; stamping ink; buttons

JOURNALING

I have a confession to make... the five years I was a waitress at Rockwell's were some of the best years of my life. Yes, my feet killed me after hours on the job. Yes, I became attached to my "regulars." Yes, I missed all the fun everyone else had in high school. No, I never got to go to a football or basketball game on a Friday night 'cause I needed the money. Yes, I even liked the nasty customers, and no, I never spit in their food. Yes, the customer is always right! Yes, I am a very good tipper now and almost always leave 20%. Yes, I would do it again in a heartbeat if I needed to.

The Story Behind the Layout

The chores were finished and my husband was fed.
    I'm in my jammies, and the kids are in bed.

I checked on the boards and saw a big hit
    for reality pages, I knew I'd submit.

I grabbed the photo boxes and opened the lids,
    I found some stuff from before I had kids.

Working all night, I had lots of fun!
    My scraps came together and my layout was done!

AMANDA WILLIAMS

★ Tumacacori, Arizona

I started scrapbooking after my engagement in 1999. I have been married to my husband, Josh, for six years, and we have two young daughters. I spend my days caring for our girls and our cat named Mouse. At night, I unwind with my trimmer, patterned papers and double-sided tape. My other loves include dancing, Diet Coke and my husband's practical jokes. My plans for the future include taking step aerobic classes, mentoring young moms and having another child.

MY *last* DAYDREAM

Me at the Castle Marksburg in Germany, 18, full of hopes & dreams, believing I was the beautiful heroine of my fantasy because I had my first boyfriend. I didn't journal on that day, but wrote with abandon to the boy (who later burned the letters.) I was thinking of him - a Daydream of a knight in shining armor, that mother of all daydreams. I gave myself to it, somehow knowing it would be my last chance to believe - a TRANSITIONAL MOMENT from which I moved happily into adult hood.

photo taken May 1993
journaling 2005 ♡

SARAH @ 18

MY LAST DAYDREAM

SUPPLIES:
Patterned papers (7gypsies, Captured Elements, Keeping Memories Alive); paints (DecoArt, Making Memories); vintage letters, rub-on letters, artisan label (Making Memories); decorative tape (Heidi Swapp); foil stars; cardstock

JOURNALING

Me at the Castle Marksburg in Germany, 18, full of hopes and dreams, believing I was the beautiful heroine of my fantasy because I had my first boyfriend. I didn't journal on that trip, but wrote with abandon to the boy (who later burned the letters). I was thinking of him—a daydream of a knight in shining armor—that mother of all dreams. I gave myself to it, somehow knowing it would be my last chance to believe—a transitional moment from which I moved happily into adulthood.

The Story Behind the Layout

I remember my mother taking this picture and saying, "Now, smile, Sarah. You're going to be sorry if you don't smile!" I took a stand (somewhat petulantly, I'm sure) for what I hoped was a wistful expression befitting a girl of eighteen. I was coming out of a particularly nice daydream, made possible by the reality of the castle we were visiting in Germany, and the existence of a certain surfer boy who was the recipient of all my thoughts and experiences of that trip through letters.

I have always remembered that moment and am really happy to have captured this particular photograph of myself looking back at the past, and yet headed on toward the future. The picture portrays exactly where I was standing at that time in my life. Today, life has given me all that I could hope for, certainly in different ways or different forms then I expected then. I have come to other crossroads in life, and will come to more I'm sure, as it goes on. Standing here today, looking back on that girl, I think I could tell her that she won't be disappointed, and that it's much richer, although at times difficult, and altogether better in Real Life.

SARAH HEROMAN

★ Arlington, Texas

As a child, I loved to dream, imagine and create. Now, my best dreams are my real life. I am wife to another dreamer, Bill, and the mother of two delightful children, Bo and Emma. I work part-time as a home health nurse and scrap in all of my spare moments.

Sometimes i wish i could forget my teen years. i often felt crippled with self → consciousness, my boyfriend was controlling, and my emotions seemed too strong to bear. i'm so glad that God brought me through it → i don't like remembering those years at all.

You Are Not Here ▼

YOU ARE NOT HERE

SUPPLIES:
Textured cardstock (Prism); rub-on phrase (7 gypsies); ribbons (Offray); pens (American Crafts, Sanford Corp.)

JOURNALING

Sometimes I wish I could forget my teen years. I often felt crippled with self-consciousness, my boyfriend was controlling, and my emotions seemed too strong to bear. I'm so glad that God brought me through it; I don't like remembering those years at all.

The Story Behind the Layout

Being such a sentimental person, I usually love rooting through boxes of old photos. I came across a box of things from high school, and did not enjoy looking at them at all. I wanted to stuff everything back in the box and pretend it wasn't there. This page came from that experience. I know that stage of life helped mold my character into what it is today, and I am grateful for that, but I'm so thankful that phase of my life is over.

HANNI BAUMGARDNER
★ Warsaw, Indiana

My mother used to get so frustrated with me on long car trips because I would tote along all of my art supplies. I'd create all sorts of projects and leave all the little bits in the car for her to clean up. Things haven't changed much...I still love playing with bits of paper and glue! Except now I have to clean up after myself. I've been "officially" scrapbooking for the past five or six years, and enjoy every minute of it. I scrap mostly about me, my family, my little Shih Tzu Miyagi, and everyday life here in this small midwest town!

> "THERE REALLY ISN'T AN IDEAL RELATIONSHIP, IT'S HOW YOU DEAL WITH THE IMPERFECTIONS OF THE RELATIONSHIP THAT MAKES IT IDEAL."
> UNKNOWN

MATTERS OF THE HEART >>>

The relationships in our lives define us. Each person who enters our life serves a purpose. Some give us strength, hope, courage and advice. Some teach us about love and loss. Some teach us about empathy and appreciating the differences in others. Each of these relationships has a place in our lives, our hearts and our souls. Even the most negative of relationships serves a purpose if you use it as an experience to learn a valuable lesson about yourself or others.

The deep connections we have with others are the single most important aspect of our lives. Relationships with our parents, children, families and friends shape who we are. They fill our lives with substance and serve as our support system, our strength and our base. Each relationship fulfills a different need within our soul. Some relationships are brief and some last a lifetime. With each person that enters your life, you are forever changed.

YOU AND I: WE USED TO BE FRIENDS

SUPPLIES:
Patterned papers (Amscan, Autumn Leaves, Karen Foster Design); cardstock (Paper Company); eyelets (American Tag Co.); stamps (Purple Onion Designs); rub-on letters (Bobarbo); pen

JOURNALING

A long time ago, we used to be friends. Time, space, silence separate us but dear brother—I miss you.

NATALIE BENSIMHON

★ Easton, Pennsylvania

The Story Behind the Layout

As we've gotten older, my brother and I have drifted apart. This layout always reminds me of how close we once were, how much I love my brother...and how much I miss him.

Size

does

the principal thing

MATTER

Girlfriends come in all shapes and sizes. Shannan and I are no exception to this rule. I'm tall – she's short. I'm a brunette – she's a blonde. She's petite and I'm not. In so many ways we are alike but yet different in others. Our philosophy on life is one that is the same and what defines us. While this is what connects us in many ways, we are still very different. Aside from the physical differences, she has an IQ that is far higher than mine. I respect her so much for this and what she has done with her life. With her high intellect and my large amount of useless trivia knowledge, we still connect in ways I never thought possible.

Shannan also has a heart that is larger than her petite frame can carry. She has taught me more about hospitality, forgiveness and unselfishness than anyone else. I know that I can count on her for anything from taking care of my family to forgiving me of any foolish words that I may say. She helps me expand the borders in my life and stretch my understanding and my goals to places I wish to go.

While physically we look completely different in our sizes and shapes, Shannan and I are connected for life. Shannan is small in size but large in character. When it comes to girlfriends, size does matter.

Be it ever so humble there's no place like home

THROUGH
THICK & THIN

Anything for a Quiet Life.

SIZE DOES MATTER

SUPPLIES:
Patterned papers (7 gypsies); textured cardstock (Bazzill); chipboard letters (Li'l Davis Designs); rub-on letters (Jeneva & Company); paint (Krylon); canvas (Fredrix Artist Canvas); rub-on stitches, phrase sticker (7 gypsies); distress ink (Ranger)

JOURNALING

Girlfriends come in all shapes and sizes. Shannan and I are no exception to this rule. I'm tall—she's short. I'm a brunette—she's a blonde. She's petite and I'm not. In so many ways we are alike but yet different in others. Our philosophy on life is one that is the same and what defines us. While this is what connects us in many ways, we are still very different. Aside from the physical differences, she has an IQ that is far higher than mine. I respect her so much for this and what she has done with her life. With her high intellect and my large amount of useless trivia knowledge, we still connect in ways I never thought possible. Shannan also has a heart that is larger than her petite frame can carry. She has taught me more about hospitality, forgiveness and unselfishness than anyone else. I know that I can count on her for anything from taking care of my family, to forgiving me of any foolish words that I may say. She helps me expand the borders in my life and stretches my understanding and my goals to places I wish to go. While physically we look completely different in our sizes and shapes, Shannan and I are connected for life. Shannan is small in size but large in character. When it comes to girlfriends, size does matter.

The Story Behind the Layout

My best friend Shannan and I could not look more different if we tried. When people ask if we are sisters, we give each other an odd "are they kidding?" look. I wanted to do a page about our physical differences and our shared life values.

KITTY FOSTER

★ Snellville, Georgia

I've been writing, designing and teaching in the scrapbooking field since 2000. I have been fortunate to be published in many scrapbook magazines and idea books and to be featured in an ongoing article in *Scrapbooking and Beyond*. I have designed for several companies, and I am currently designing for Fancy Pants Designs and Creative Imaginations. When not scrapbooking, you can often find me taking photographs on the sideline of one of my kid's sporting events, wearing funky jeans or reading a book.

DO YOU BELIEVE IN FATE?

SUPPLIES:

Patterned paper (American Crafts); bamboo paper (Magic Scraps); textured cardstock (Bazzill); letter stickers (Staples); metal hinges, mini brads (Making Memories); epoxy sticker (Creative Imaginations); decorative tape (Heidi Swapp); staples

JOURNALING

Do you believe in fate? A detour traced back to one singular moment? Something seemingly insignificant that completely changed the course of your life? My life definitely changed on October 20. That is the day I met Jonathan. Of course I thought he was a hottie the second I saw him. Of course I had our entire wedding planned as soon as he introduced himself. Of course! Except for one tiny detail. He was 18. And he wasn't interested. I cut my losses and moved on. We remained friends and hung out occasionally in the next year. I continued to have a secret crush on him the entire time. Loved him. And finally one day, it happened. We hooked up. Now my life is nothing like I ever imagined. We are now married (something I swore would never happen and I'd be a spinster with 50 cats). I have purpose in my life. Something I never had before my amazing husband. I have realized there is a reason for things. God does have a plan. Maybe not always on the same time table as yours, or in the ways that you want...but always the way you need.

The Story Behind the Layout

I wanted to create a layout that summed up the events of my life in this stage. How things that I thought happened for no reason did indeed have a purpose. How I thought my life was random and haphazard, but the events all actually ended up coinciding. How my life has been guided by fate. I focused on a specific date because it was the day I met my husband. That is when all the little bits began to fall in place, even though I had no idea at that time.

102000

KRISTINA CONTES

★ Ronkonkoma, New York

I have been a lover of all things art my whole life, but have only recently discovered the world that is scrapping. I love that there is a way to document my life in such a creative manner. Being able to let my feelings and voice just flow onto my pages feels so good! My style is definitely a little out of the ordinary, but I love that there is enough room in this industry to let everyone have a voice. I think it's important to make pages that are unique to you and your ideas, and to capture every little bit of this fleeting life that you can. And I also think you should have fun while doing it!

CRAZY

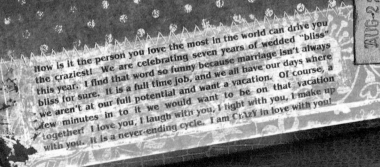

HUSBAND & Wife

POST CARD
Universal Postal Union

AUG 22 2005

in love

united in life ~ two become one

How is it the person you love the most in the world can drive you the craziest! We are celebrating seven years of wedded "bliss" this year. I find that word so funny because marriage isn't always bliss for sure. It is a full time job, and we all have our days where we aren't at our full potential and want a vacation. Of course, a few minutes in to it we would want to be on that vacation together! I love you, I laugh with you, I fight with you, I make up with you. It is a never-ending cycle. I am CRAZY in love with you!

CRAZY IN LOVE

SUPPLIES:
Patterned papers (Autumn Leaves, K&Company); postcard (7 gypsies); rub-on letters, elements (BasicGrey, My Mind's Eye); wooden letters, letter stamps (Stampin' Up!): foam alphabet stamps, mini brad, acrylic paint (Making Memories); distress ink (Ranger); ribbon (Morex Corp.); jute (Provo Craft); silk flower; thread

The Story Behind the Layout

I created this layout after a disagreement with my husband, Ryan. He has a way of getting my blood boiling in no time and then making everything all right again with just a few words. No one else gets to me the way he does. Of course, I tell him no one else would be crazy enough to put up with him, but as much as I hate to admit it, the same is probably true for me. We both know neither of us is perfect and our crazy quirks complement each other perfectly!

JOURNALING

How is it the person you love the most in the world can drive you the craziest? We are celebrating seven years of wedded "bliss" this year. I find that word so funny because marriage isn't always bliss for sure. It is a full-time job, and we all have our days where we aren't at our full potential and want a vacation. Of course, a few minutes in to it we would want to be on that vacation together! I love you, I laugh with you, I fight with you, I make up with you. It is a never-ending cycle. I am Crazy in love with you!

SUMMER FORD

★ Bulverde, Texas

I am a stay-at-home mom to three wild things that most other people call my children. Holt, Hunter and our baby girl, Hannah, keep me running everywhere! I have been married to my college sweetheart and best friend in the world, Ryan, for almost eight years, and we have made our home in the beautiful Texas hill country. When I am not scrapbooking or stamping, I enjoy home improvement, decorating and organizing.

the
SPACE
between

is where you'll find me hiding, waiting for you

LOVE IS ALL WE NEED HERE

THE SPACE BETWEEN

SUPPLIES:
Patterned paper (BasicGrey); cardstock (Bazzill): rub-on letters (Making Memories); die-cut circles (Sizzix); foam alphabet stamps (Heidi Swapp); distress ink (Ranger)

The Story Behind the Layout

For a few months in 2005, I saw the first real marriage problems that my husband and I ever had during our seven years of marriage. Until that point, we had what some would call the "perfect marriage."

After this period, we finally reached our breakthrough point and things changed and improved. We began to repair our marriage. One night while away on a trip, I heard this Dave Matthews Band song and knew that it was perfect for our situation. We had experienced an almost permanent space between us, but we pulled through it together and more in love than ever before. The lyrics rang true and spoke to my heart that night and I came home and made this layout.

JOURNALING

March and April of 2005, Drew and I saw our first real marriage problems. We had both just been through huge, life-changing events. Unfortunately, how he coped was by distancing himself from those he loved, namely me. He was cold, he was distant. Eventually, I had enough and I left. I told him things had to change and gave him time to think, and I came home. And then he did it again...only worse. My heart broke into a million pieces and I again left. I bought and filled out separation papers and told him that his change would have to come now or never. He didn't shed a tear, he didn't do anything. Then on a Saturday he finally broke down. He sobbed for everything that he put Roslyn and I through and for everything that he did. He promised that he would be better. And he has. He has grown into even more of a loving and attentive husband and father. He is the person that I always knew he was. He just had to remember and believe that that was there inside of him the whole time... because I did. Through it all, the heartbreak, the uncertainty and the pain, I knew that we would get through it. Better, stronger and more in love than ever before.

RACHEL HALL

★ Prescott, Arizona

I was born and raised in the small town of Prescott, Arizona, and reside there to this day. I married my husband when I was seventeeen years old, and we have been married for seven years, and have one daughter, Roslyn. I'm a stay-at-home mom and work part-time at our local scrapbook store designing and teaching classes. My passions include scrapbooking, history, art, writing, photography and raising my family. My aim is to one day have a history degree, with an emphasis in Women's Studies. I am constantly seeing beauty in the world around me. My goal is to share this beauty with others, mainly my daughter.

if
it's
over
let it go
and
come
tomorrow
it will
seem

SO

YESTERDAY

im gonna be

okay

hold
on
to
the

memories

*LIFE
HAPPENS

2005

2-5

the hardest part
of the breakup was knowing it was the
right thing for me and still hurting so
badly. it took months of tears and pain before
it seemed "so yesterday" i spent 2 years with
the man i thought i'd wed. that hurts but im gonna be okay

SO YESTERDAY

SUPPLIES:
Patterned papers (American Crafts, Provo Craft, SEI); textured cardstock (Bazzill); ribbon, letter stickers, pen (American Crafts); photo corners, chipboard flowers (Heidi Swapp); decorative brads (Making Memories); rub-on elements (Doodlebug Design, Heidi Swapp); label maker (DYMO)

JOURNALING

The hardest part of the breakup was knowing that it was the right thing for me and still hurting so badly. It took months of tears and pain before it seemed "so yesterday." I spent two years with the man I thought I'd wed. That hurts. But I'm gonna be okay.

The Story Behind the Layout

I will admit to being an avid Hilary Duff fan. The lyrics to her song "So Yesterday" were filled with just enough girl power to inspire me to scrapbook a painful breakup. When my long-term relationship filled with broken promises finally ended, I knew it was the right thing...but the pain that followed left me heartbroken and confused. Knowing I had done what was best for me didn't ease the pain of the loss. As a result, I held onto the hope of reconciliation for far too long and sunk further and further into misery. I was so full of doubt in myself, in God, and in the idea of love. I had built my life around the unfulfilled promises of a man and when that man couldn't deliver, I was completely shaken. I spent many restless nights in tears, wondering how I could ever trust anyone else, let alone fall in love again. Eventually, the pain began to subside. Good began to replace the bad. Hurtful memories no longer invaded my mind at every turn. And I learned to trust again. I learned to trust myself. I learned to trust God. I learned to trust in love. And eventually, I learned to trust another man. And it was surprisingly easy. In part because the words to a Hilary Duff song were true: "If it's over let it go, and come tomorrow it will seem so yesterday, haven't you heard that I'm gonna be okay."

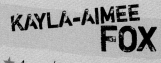

KAYLA-AIMEE FOX

★ Acworth, Georgia

I am currently in my senior year of college, pursuing a degree in Sociology and Organizational Management. I enjoy scrapbooking, cream sodas, my middle name and getting surprise packages in the mail. I can most likely be found pouring over wedding magazines or writing "Mrs. Kayla-Aimee Terrell" on scrap pieces of paper, as I am engaged to marry my favorite person in the world on December 22, 2006.

That you would be the one to
teach me patience.
That I would never
That I would ge
after you di
mommy!"
That I wo
just to m
That you
a better
That I
you bre
That yo

What I didn't know...

THE MIRACLE OF
MOTHERHOOD >>>

"THE MOST IMPORTANT THING SHE'D LEARNED OVER THE YEARS WAS THAT THERE WAS NO WAY TO BE A PERFECT MOTHER AND A MILLION WAYS TO BE A GOOD ONE."
JILL CHURCHILL

Motherhood is the most amazing experience you will ever have, and yet the toughest undertaking you will ever face. A mother wears many hats: teacher, nurse, guidance counselor, disciplinarian, coach, cheerleader, cook, maid, referee, and in the adult years of a child, friend. She is selfless, caring and nurturing. She feels her children's pain, she lives her children's successes and mourns their failures. As a mother, there is endless worry and wonder, "Am I doing this right?"

To the child, a mother is the center of their universe. Their little lives are wrapped around her. Once you are a mother, you will always be a mother…the role is infinite. The responsibility is massive, but the rewards are endless.

WHAT I DIDN'T KNOW...

SUPPLIES:
Patterned paper (My Mind's Eye); textured cardstock (Bazzill); thread

JOURNALING

That you would be the one to teach me patience.
That I would never stop worrying, ever.
That I would get my ears pierced at 35 after you did and said, "It didn't hurt, mommy!"
That I would make a fool of myself just to make you laugh.
That you would make me want to be a better person.
That I would lay awake listening to you breathe.
That you would be my only child.
I love you.

The Story Behind the Layout

We imagined how it would be to have a child, and finally having Lena turned our whole world upside down. There were a lot of things we'd heard from friends who had kids and from books—but what it's really like…we didn't know.

DAGMAR NEUMANN

★ Gilroy, California

I am originally from Germany, and I have lived in the United States for three years. I started scrapbooking three months after we moved here, and I am hooked. When I'm not scrapbooking, I like to read, cook and spend time with my family.

BeLLY

worship. (wûr'shĭp) noun. 1. The reverent love and devotion accorded a sacred object. 2. To honor and love. 3. To regard with ardent or adoring esteem or devotion. 4. love unquestioningly and uncritically or to excess.

miracle... in progress

WORSHiP

it's amazing how much my body can change in just 10 months, but I admit that when I'm pregnant is one of the few times I love & appreciate my body - just a miracle!

BELLY WORSHIP

SUPPLIES:
Patterned papers (7gypsies, Creative Imaginations, KI Memories, Memories, Paper Adventures, Rusty Pickle); chipboard letters (Heidi Swapp); other letter embellishments (Wal-Mart); chalk ink (Clearsnap); acrylic paint; transparency; pens; ribbon; staples

JOURNALING

It's amazing how much my body can change in just 10 months, but I admit that when I'm pregnant is one of the few times I love & appreciate my body—just a miracle!

The Story Behind the Layout

I have body issues. Doesn't every woman? Mine are a bit intermittent, as I do sometimes think that I'm pretty smokin' for a mom-type. But on most days, I feel like the typical haus frau, decked out in jeans and T-shirts, with my hair in a haphazard ponytail. But when I'm pregnant, none of that matters. The mythical "pregnancy glow" becomes reality (at least in my head), and I love my body as it goes through the miraculous process of growing a new life. I waver between marveling at the wonder of how my body can achieve this phenomenon and secretly fearing the reality of just how big my huge belly will get before being criss-crossed with stretch marks.

This picture was taken at 37 weeks of pregnancy with my daughter Tayvan. I walked around with one hand constantly on my belly, rubbing the growing bump in some instinctual way of communicating with my unborn baby. Everyone, from my husband to random people at the mall, wanted to touch my belly. It was the be-all-end-all of conversation for the entire ten months. For the layout, I wanted to give it an overall grungy but pink feel without screaming patterns, so I chose soft pinks and heavily inked them so that you get the gradations of color for interest without the patterns becoming a focal point of the piece. Because the focus is all about The Belly!

STACI ETHERIDGE

★ McKinney Texas

I'm still a girl at heart. Luckily, I married the man that knew me when I really was still a girl, my junior-high sweetheart, Bobby. We've been married for nine years and have been fortunate enough to have a crew of three great kids: Lillian, my sassy daughter, Declan, my sweet son, and Tayvan, my always-smiling baby daughter. It's one of the first things I think about when I wake up, and the thing that keeps me from going to bed at night. But that's all right because I love it...paper, ink, alphas, embellishments, etc. I love to collect, love to play, and I love to create! I'm a hardcore scrappin' fiend.

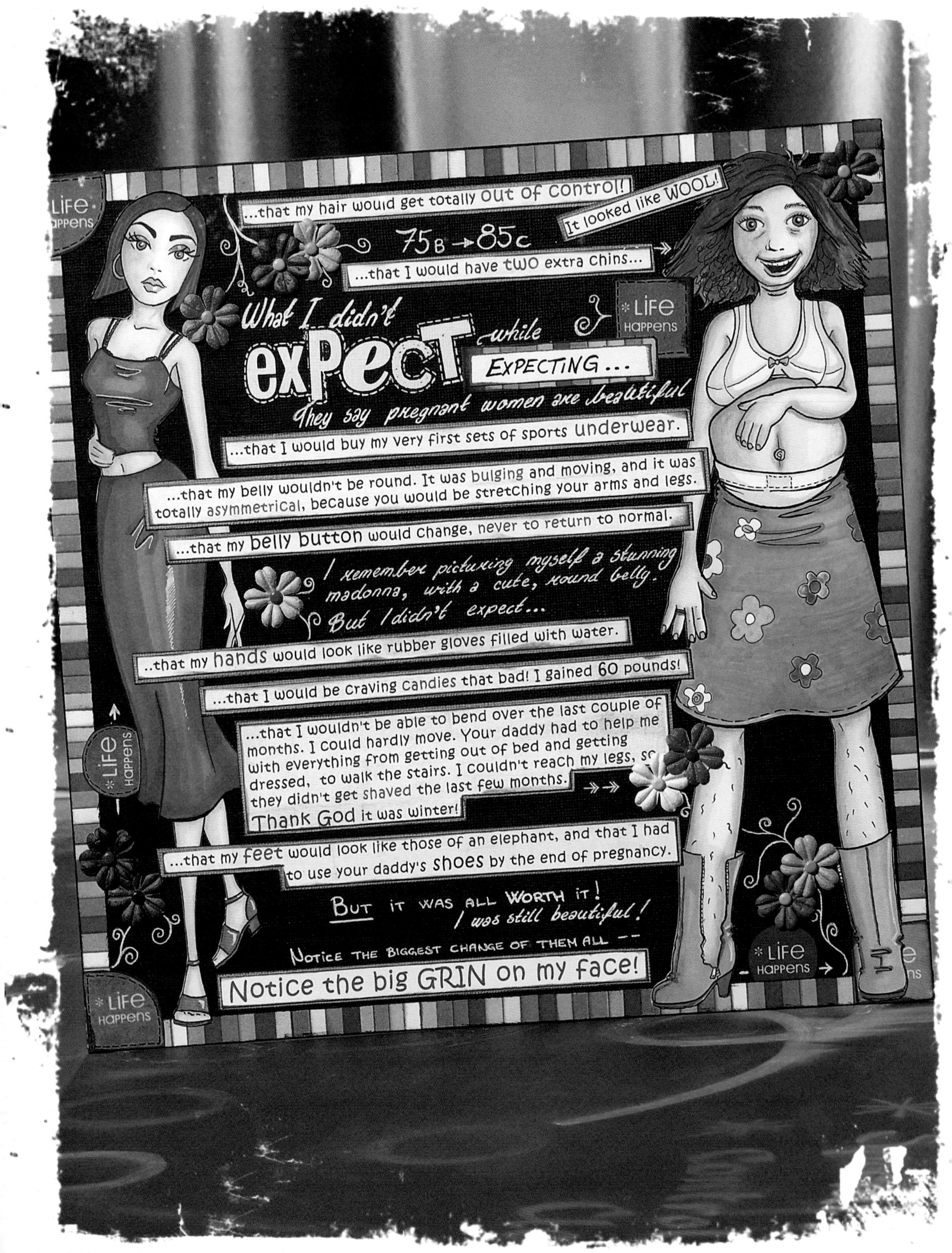

LIFE HAPPENS
...that my hair would get totally out of control!
It looked like WOOL!
75B → 85C
...that I would have two extra chins...
What I didn't expect while expecting...
LIFE HAPPENS
They say pregnant women are beautiful
...that I would buy my very first sets of sports underwear.
...that my belly wouldn't be round. It was bulging and moving, and it was totally asymmetrical, because you would be stretching your arms and legs.
...that my belly button would change, never to return to normal.
I remember picturing myself a stunning madonna, with a cute, round belly. But I didn't expect...
..that my hands would look like rubber gloves filled with water.
...that I would be craving candies that bad! I gained 60 pounds!
...that I wouldn't be able to bend over the last couple of months. I could hardly move. Your daddy had to help me with everything from getting out of bed and getting dressed, to walk the stairs. I couldn't reach my legs, so they didn't get shaved the last few months.
Thank God it was winter!
LIFE HAPPENS
...that my feet would look like those of an elephant, and that I had to use your daddy's shoes by the end of pregnancy.
But it was all worth it!
I was still beautiful!
Notice the biggest change of them all --
Notice the big GRIN on my face!
LIFE HAPPENS
LIFE HAPPENS

WHAT I DIDN'T EXPECT WHILE EXPECTING

SUPPLIES:

Patterned paper (Provo Craft); textured cardstocks (Bazzill, SEI); gel pens (EK Success, Pentel); colored pencils (EK Success); markers (Letraset); chalk ink (Clearsnap); rub-on letters, mini brads (Making Memories); paper flowers (Prima)

The Story Behind the Layout

Like many scrapbookers, I'm not too fond of having my photo taken. That's why I ended up having almost no pregnancy shots of myself. One of the happiest, most life-changing times of my life, and I didn't get it on film! Browsing other people's galleries and albums, I've seen so many gorgeous pregnancy layouts, and I so regret not taking those pictures while I had the chance. As my layout shows, I didn't feel much like the stunning, radiant, pregnant woman you'd usually hear—or read—about. I thought the best way to document how I felt was by drawing some "self portraits." Not feeling beautiful, or not looking all that stunning, really didn't matter. I had never experienced such happiness before, and I want to remember those months forever.

MALIN T PETTERSON

★ Baerum, Norway

I've been married to Jarle for the last seven years, with whom I have a three-year-old daughter, Alida, and two teenage stepsons. I've been scrapbooking for three years, but have been doing art and crafts for as long as I can remember. I've also taught classes in scrapbooking, card making and stamping over the last few years. I'm active in several online scrapbooking communities, and love having the opportunity to share my passion for scrapbooking with friends all over the world.

POSTPARTUM

CONFIDENTIAL

or

TICKET 022856

hell

So what is postpartum anyway?
I begged the doctor to let me
stay an extra day !
What makes a woman feel helpless,
not in control and always
teary eyed.

POSTPARTUM OR HELL?

SUPPLIES:
Patterned papers (source unknown); stickers (American Crafts, Leaving Prints, Pebbles); fasteners, paper flower, mini brad, rub-on element (Making Memories); stamps (Leaving Prints); photo corners; ribbon

JOURNALING

So what is postpartum anyway? I begged the doctor to let me stay an extra day. What makes a woman feel helpless, not in control and always teary eyed?

The Story Behind the Layout

After having six prior deliveries and never having postpartum ordeals, I thought that I was in the clear for the postpartum after my twins were born. Was I wrong! I am not sure if it was having a C-section that made it worse for me, or if it was simply due to the hormones of having twins. Whatever the case, it surely was a double batch of crazy emotions that I needed to fight to overcome. I had just watched Brooke Shields on a morning show and heard her story, so I was aware of what I may need. This layout was done at the end of my three-month up-and-down roller coaster ride. It was great therapy and helped me organize each feeling I had in each product that I used.

The ticket stands for the ticket to hell. The bra latches are representing me trying to hold it together as a woman and a wife. The tape represents me trying to hold the house together. The four photo corners represent me trying to hold myself together. The upper-right corner picture shows how we can go about daily living though we feel we are in a window showing the nakedness and how nothing is quite right. The chopped journaling/lettering are how we are not able to discuss it. The hand and heart on the top of the frame represents the caring "women" who see and care and also come to help us while we are in need. The two circles at the bottom (opposite side of hell) represents the fun colors of life peeking through to show that the good side is there and obtainable.

KAREN CLARK

★ Rice Lake, Wisconsin

I am a happily married wife to Dan and an at-home mother. We have been given gifts of eight wonderful children. They are my life. That is why I scrapbook.

MOTHERHOOD

SUPPLIES:
Patterned papers (American Crafts, BasicGrey, K&Company, Provo Craft); textured cardstocks (Bazzill, Die Cuts With A View); mesh (Magic Mesh); letter stickers (American Crafts); rub-on letters (Li'l Davis Designs); colored staples (Making Memories); pen; decorative scissors (Fiskars); acrylic paint

The Story Behind the Layout

I love to document the chaos of my everyday life because I think that is what my kids are going to remember. Photographing the fun stuff like silly T-shirts and favorite toys adds variety to my scrapbooks and captures the trends of the times.

JOURNALING

Motherhood = comedy + conflict. Laughter + tears... never ending "pull my finger" novelties – 101 crappy attitudes, crap all over the house, yelling, whining, teasing, a stomach turning fear of the unknown, unpredictable hours – unforeseen circumstances – risk – pride and sometimes even disappointment.

ALECIA GRIMM

★ Atlanta, Georgia

I am a spirited artist living in downtown Atlanta, Georgia, originally from the frozen tundra of North Dakota. I am married and have four kids who keep me on my toes. I've been scrapbooking, painting and creating art journals for almost ten years. I am fascinated with photos and the process of narrating everyday life through art. I thrive on challenge, and strive to be an innovative, design driven, mixed-media artist.

When I am not scrapbooking, I enjoy going on road trips, drinking strong coffee, reading nonfiction, painting, listening to an eclectic mix of music, and spending time with family.

Life LESSONS

WHAT THE PARENTING BOOKS DON'T TELL YOU!

1. Just because something is childproof, doesn't mean it's Matthew-proof.

2. Putting something up high is not a deterrent, it's a challenge.

3. Eating cat food will not kill you. (but it will make your breath stink.)

4. Older brothers are the best bad examples.

5. The bigger the audience, the larger the tantrum.

WHAT THE PARENTING BOOKS DON'T TELL YOU

SUPPLIES:
Patterned paper (K&Company); cardstock (Bazzill); chipboard letters (Heidi Swapp, Li'l Davis Designs); rub-on elements (Autumn Leaves); metal mesh (Making Memories); label maker (DYMO); decoupage medium (Plaid); chalk ink (Clearsnap)

JOURNALING

1. Just because something is childproof, doesn't mean it's Matthew-proof.

2. Putting something up high is not a deterrent, it's a challenge.

3. Eating cat food will not kill you (but it will make your breath stink).

4. Older brothers are the best bad examples.

5. The bigger the audience, the larger the tantrum.

The Story Behind the Layout

This is the reality of parenting. Every parenting book I ever read scared me senseless with all the precautions they advised. The result was that my first-born was rather coddled and protected until his first brother came along. (And boy, was that an adjustment!) Gradually, I relaxed, and by the time I got to number three, I knew which things were true emergencies and which were something to just deal with and go on. I also learned that the youngest gets into the most trouble because he:

a.) has the best teachers (big brothers)

b.) has to compete to make his mark in the family.

So, when I saw Matthew devouring cat food, all I could do was laugh, grab a camera and then go brush his teeth! Children have to be resilient to put up with their parent's mistakes (and their own!). Otherwise, they'd never survive to adulthood!

JULIE MARTINEZ

★ Orlando, Florida

I am a mother of three stinky boys and a wife to a Musketeer. I work in the hospitality industry in Orlando, Florida, but aspire to be a stay-at-home mommy. I'm originally from San Angelo, Texas, and will always be a Texas girl at heart. I started scrapping after the birth of my first child in 1999 when my mother gifted me with supplies. (Thanks, Mom!) It's been an addiction ever since, and I truly consider it worth it when my boys look at their books.

ating cat food will not

kill you.

ake your breath stink.)

overwhelmed
talentless
grumpy
depressed
taken for granted
resigned
exhausted
ignored
fat
frustrated
envious
brainless
unappreciated
left out
grouchy
inadequate

MOMMY GETS
cranky

MOMMY GETS CRANKY

SUPPLIES:
Cardstock (Bazzill); rub-on letters (Autumn Leaves); letter stickers (American Crafts); stamping ink (Tsukineko)

JOURNALING

To whom it may concern:

I'm beat. I'm bled dry by the three people under my care. I try to give myself a little creative time to boost my spirit, but there are either interruptions or I start so late in the day that inspiration escapes me. I watch those around me manage to cook dinner or have a clean house or play with their kids or have a girls' night out or a date night with hubby or get to be involved in scrapping opportunities, and I'm left to wonder what I'm doing wrong. I had big plans for a layout about real life, but time eluded me and now I'm throwing a page together, hoping it's enough. Cool techniques? Amazing art? Fuhgeddaboutit.

I've come to the conclusion that motherhood is a conspiracy against women to keep us so exhausted and insane that we can't organize our thoughts much less a revolution. What my life has become is something I no longer recognize. And the irony is that it is a good life. A great one, actually. I'm in love with my husband, I adore my children, and I know that I'm actually NOT talentless or unappreciated or ignored. Yet that's the way I feel at the end of the day when I realize that somewhere in the past 12 hours life has passed me by.

Yes, I tend to get a little cranky by the end of the day. And will I get this layout done on time? Probably not. But at least I'll have accomplished something for ME. And maybe this layout isn't filled with amazing techniques, but it is filled with the words that best describe my reality. And really, isn't reality nothing but the truth? There you go. I'm set.

The Story Behind the Layout

When I heard the call for "real life" layouts, I got so excited. Finally, a page call that seemed tailor-made for me! I immediately got the idea for a page about how life and motherhood are not always perfect. I recently blogged on this very topic and figured my words would work perfectly for the layout. I just needed a photo.

For a couple of weeks life conspired against me, never giving me free time to set up the tripod. Or if I had time, it was a day when I hadn't showered. The more I delayed doing the layout, the crankier I got, thinking here was the one shot to do something great and authentic and possibly get published.

The day the layout was due I was exhausted and worn out, but it occurred to me that if I was going to do a page about the overwhelming aspects of life and motherhood, a photo of me looking clean and rested and happy wouldn't be right. So I set up the tripod and went at it, snapping photos of me looking grungy, tired, frustrated. There it was. Reality. The words were there, the photos were just right, the angst was simmering below the surface. Me. Now. The truth. And under deadline.

MICHELE SKINNER

★ Burnsville, Minnesota

I was bitten by the scrap bug in 2001, after a year of searching for baby books that weren't full of licensed characters or that assumed family trees had normal branches. I am a writer and editor by trade, but I am currently a stay-home mommy to my son, Henry, and daughter, Harper. I live with my gorgeous kids and genius geek husband, Marc.

MAMA-HOOD

MEANS

* I get to watch you
grow * dirty
diapers * dirty
dishes *

THE GLORY

sleepless
nights * lots of kisses
* stray cars on the
stairs * worry *
headaches * I have
another guy in my life
who likes to hold my
hand * messes

* a lot of
feedings *
pockets full of
rocks * a fridge
covered in truck
magnets * a stained
couch * a full heart *

INSIGHTS

if I've told you... | pipe down
you'll p...
sit down
settle down

grow up   sit up
you're the best kid ever | put that down
you're my favorite | ignore them, they're just jealous | go ask your father

MAMA-HOOD

SUPPLIES:
Patterned papers (Autumn Leaves, Scenic Route Paper Co., We R Memory Keepers); chipboard letters (Heidi Swapp, We R Memory Keepers); letter stickers, brads (American Crafts); stickers, tags (7gypsies); letters (K&Company); chalk ink (Clearsnap); colored staples (Making Memories); paper flowers (Prima); ribbon; note cards; felt; fabric; clip

JOURNALING

Mama-hood means:

- I get to watch you grow
- dirty diapers
- dirty dishes
- a lot of feedings
- pockets full of rocks
- a fridge covered in truck magnets
- a stained couch
- a full heart
- sleepless nights
- lots of kisses
- stray cars on the stairs
- worry headaches
- I have another guy in my life who likes to hold my hand
- messes

The Story Behind the Layout

I wanted this layout to convey my feelings on motherhood, particularly how my life has changed since I became a mother. All my minutes, hours, days, weeks and months are full of my son. I'm so grateful for that. I'm grateful that I can't do the wash without finding a rock or two in his pockets. I'm grateful that there's another man in my life who likes to hold my hand. I'm even grateful for the sleepless nights and the trips to the ER, because they've taught me compassion, humility and endless love. I have mama-hood and my sweet son to thank for that.

HEATHER BURCH

★ Logan, Utah

I started playing with paper and embellishments about a year ago after my son was born. When I saw his tiny face for the first time, I felt this need to preserve his story—OUR story. In the beginning, I found this hobby gave me more than preserved memories. It gave me a creative outlet—a part of my life that was just mine. I'm having a great time submitting my work for contests and publication. I've had some success, but the best part is the company my husband and I started called Poppy Ink. We've become passionate about bringing the latest products and techniques to the public. It's been a wild ride, and I can't wait for what's to come!

dYRtY secrets
A STAY AT HOME MOM'S CONFESSIONS

1. i DO get tIreD oF reAdinG tHe sAme DAmN stOryBookS OVER & OVER.

2. I sTay in mY JaMmieSmosT dAys-WHY NOT? i raRElygo anYwHEre.

3. averGing 4 hOurs oF... sLeeP a niGHt SUCKS ass.

4. i always UseD to tHink Dressing iDEntical twins aliKe was DorkY-now i THiNk it's CUTE.

5. i beCome tongUe-tieD during aDult cOnverSations-tRying to aVoiD refErring to Myself in the 3rD perSon.

6. i yank DiRty cLotHes out of tHe hamPer & pErfoRm the ''SniFf TesT'' ratHer thAn do ANOTHER loaD of laUhdry.

7. occaSsionaLly, i811 dO eThan's hOmewoRk, to aVoid figHting & arGuing wiTh him To gEt it dOne.

8. i eAt the LEftoVers ofF my kiD's plaTes.

9. i cAn do a LOT of hOuseWork in tHe 30 miNutes be4 your husBanD comes homE frOm worK.

10. i hAve a *MAD* kRush on steVe fRom ''blUe's cLues''.

somEtimes-i wiLL *faKe* a siCk Day.

DONT TELL DONT TELL

Shhkhhhh!

My badH!

DIRTY LITTLE SECRETS

SUPPLIES:
Patterned papers (7 gypsies, Urban Lily); pre-printed transparency (Creative Imaginations); die-cut letters, foam stamps (KI Memories); acrylic letters, shapes (Heidi Swapp); floral stamp (Hero Arts); label maker (DYMO); colored staples, rub-on letters (Making Memories); sequins (Hero Arts, vintage); ribbons (Maya Road, May Arts, Offray); glitter (Art Institute Glitter); stamps (Stamp Craft); solvent ink (Tsukineko); pen (Sanford Corp.)

The Story Behind the Layout

As a stay-at-home mom to six beautiful children for the past four years, I've developed several "coping mechanisms" to make it possible to slip in some precious "me" time into my average day. Quite a few of my days are spent in a mind-dulling routine. To preserve my sanity, I use some of my secrets to break up the endless cycle of cleaning, laundry, and piles of paperwork that overtake my household. I may never hold the title of "Supermom" (heck, some days I don't even manage to feel like a good mom). But, as long as the kids are fed, have clothes on, and I've managed to control my temper, I feel I've done my job. My "secrets" list makes it possible for me to find a few moments throughout my day to create art, which in turn, makes me a healthier, happier person. And as my children can attest to, happy mom = happy kids. I hope years from now, when my little ones are grown, they can look back upon this page and know that mom's "Dirty Little Secrets" have benefited us all.

JUDI VANVAKINBURGH

★ Niagra Falls, New York

Being the daughter of a music teacher and an art teacher, you would think that I have been creative all my life, but you'd be wrong. I only leapt into this obsession known as scrapbooking two short years ago. I've yet to completely embrace one true style, but I hope to capture the essence of real life with my creations.

Straight up, my main inspiration is my family... my fiancé, Charlie, my step daughters Amanda and Brittany, and my children, Ethan, Eddie, Caroline and Charlotte (twins!). While I create my fair share of typical event pages, I'd say my most satisfying layouts are the ones documenting the reality of our lives, such as Eddie's diagnosis of autism. I want my children to embrace all of their history, the good and the bad.

BE ASTOUNDED!

BE AMAZED!

The Chef

I try to cook, but you see
I don't always follow the recipe.
Sometimes the food is good. But other times it's not.
Thank goodness for the Pizza Place.
They deliver - 30 minutes - fresh and hot!

The Cleaning Lady

Cleaning is not my favorite thing to do.
But neither is stepping in a pile of goo.
The nasty stuff gets cleaned right away.
But little messes wait for another day.
In short, I clean what I must...
but I don't do windows and I never ever dust.

Ms. Fix-it

This is the hat I wear when something is broke.
I research, I wonder, I prod and I poke.
It's too expensive to have a repairman come.
So I usually try to fix things some.
I've replaced a fuse and fixed the sink.
I can repair almost anything - I think!

The Jester

My kids are young and they like to have fun
I keep them laughing with a joke or a pun
It's most fun to clown around when bedtime is near.
Their giggles before sleep are music to my ear.

The Artist

The artist hat is the hat of my dreams.
But there's never enough time for art it seems.
So in stolen moments - between cleaning and cooking...
I draw and I scrap while no one is looking.

-Me?-

HAVING THE TIME OF MY LIFE

Don't ever feel bad for me. I'm living my life happily.
Being a single mom can be tough.
But my policy is "Don't sweat the small stuff."

AS THE SINGLE MOTHER JUGGLES HER MANY HATS!

THE SINGLE MOTHER'S MANY HATS

SUPPLIES:
Patterned paper (Provo Craft); cardstock (Georgia-Pacific, Paper Company); stamping ink; drawings (artist's own)

The Story Behind the Layout

Many times when I tell people that I am a single mom, their first reaction is to feel sorry for me. I just want people to know that they don't need to feel that way. I'm having a great life. Yeah, there's some extra work that I have to do, but I don't mind. My kids are my joy. My family life is filled with fun and laughter. This is a good life!

One of the biggest elements of my reality is my love of creating. So to give the most accurate reflection of my life, I thought it would be a good idea to include some of my own creations in this layout. I drew and painted all the hats as well as created the rhymes for each.

NATALIE BENSIMHON

★ Easton, Pennsylvania

I can tell you that I was born in 1966. It will be quicker for you to do the math than for me to gear up the courage to tell you my age.

I am a single mother of two children who provide me with a wealth of material to use for my scrapbooking. If it's not a funny thing they've said, then there's a stolen glance that I catch on camera. Their lives are my paints and scrapbooking paper is often my canvas.

The kids are also the subject matter of my drawings, doodles and stories. I am an artist at heart. I love to come up with ideas and really make something of them. As I look at my life today and in the future, I always hope to see a creative person toiling at some project or another.

Confessions of a...

SLACKER MOM

the shocking truth!?

i've fed the kids cereal for supper just so i could scrap. & even worse— they had to fix it... i've forgotten to bathe them for two nights in a row— yes, the "smelly kid" syndrome was my fault. i've taken them to the grocery store in houseshoes because i was too lazy to find REAL shoes. i've let them wear pajamas all day long— more times than i can count. (i wore mine too...)

CONFESSIONS OF A SLACKER MOM

SUPPLIES:
Cardstock (Stampin' Up!); photo corners, decorative tape, rub-on elements (Heidi Swapp); diamond stamp, acrylic paint (Making Memories); fabric letter tabs (Scrapworks); wooden letters (Wal-Mart); stamping ink; rhinestones; CD

JOURNALING

I've fed the kids cereal for supper just so I could scrap & even worse, they had to fix it... I've forgotten to bathe them for two nights in a row—yes, the "smelly kid" syndrome was my fault. I've taken them to the grocery store in house shoes because I was too lazy to find REAL shoes. I've let them wear pajamas all day long more times than I can count (yes, I wore mine too).

The Story Behind the Layout

Being a mom isn't easy. Just ask anyone who is a mother. Yes, it's the most rewarding, amazing experience ever, but it is still hard. And you don't get a break, or a time out, or a do-over. So my solution has been to just "slack off." Maybe it's because I'm a Gen-Xer. I think it's probably because I'm just tired. So we pull out the boxes of cereal, the fuzzy slippers and the pajama bottoms. We shuffle through our days, sometimes bathed and sometimes not. In the long run, those aren't the things that will truly make a difference in my children's lives. The difference will lie in them being able to remember a mom who was there when they needed her, who supported, encouraged and scolded when necessary, and above all, who loved them unconditionally. For me, being able to do all of those things means getting a break, taking a time out. So I slack. And we're all better off for it.

AUDREY NEAL

★ Clinton, Kentucky

I started scrapbooking in 1999 after buying a book by Becky Higgins. From the start, my pages have been grounded by a simple, linear style. However, during the past year, thanks to several amazing online scrapbooking sites, I have really formed my own style, meshing a funky/artsy vibe, with a simple foundation. I have only been scrapbooking "seriously" for the past six months or so. Ironically, very little about my work is serious. My life is chaotic and crazy, and I strive to capture that in my work. Fortunately, much of that craziness is the good kind. Laughter is a constant sound in my household, so you'll see a lot of "laugh out loud" moments in my art.

I am married to a wonderful man named Chris, and we have two beautiful daughters: Cassidy and Cameron. I teach middle and high school English and I coordinate and teach for the school district's Gifted and Talented Program.

In [THIS] pICTurE

YOU already had cancer

We DiDN'T KNOW TO BE SCaReD
We WeRe JUST goofing around
and We'LL DO it again SOON
     i PROMiSe
We WiLL FiGHT THiS Together
We WiLL BeaT THiS Thing
   YOU are NeVer alone

DeCeMBER 16 2005

[FOR] mOM

> "GOD PLACES THE HEAVIEST BURDEN ON THOSE WHO CAN CARRY ITS WEIGHT."
>
> REGGIE WHITE

LIFE LESSONS >>>

As you roll along through life, there are bound to be bumps in the road. Some of these bumps are small, and you quickly roll over them and continue on your journey. Other bumps are so significant that they unavoidably change the course of your path. We are sometimes derailed by these detours when they take us by complete surprise. Often these bumps have been there the entire time and we choose to ignore them...until one day you can no longer overlook them. The most difficult ones to deal with are the ones we least expect, the ones that find us. Those are the ones that are life changing.

Hurdles in life are a necessity. They build character, build strength...in our minds, in our souls. These hurdles teach us lessons we otherwise wouldn't have learned, and they allow us to appreciate the things we have. We could not fully appreciate the good times without experiencing the bad. It allows us to grow as a person, to realize our strengths, to understand the meaning of life, and to truly understand those who love and care about us. How you handle these bumps is up to you.

IN THIS PICTURE

SUPPLIES:
Patterned papers (Anna Griffin, Autumn Leaves); paper flower, photo corner, ribbon (Making Memories); rub-on letters (7gypsies, Making Memories); pen; stamping ink

The Story Behind the Layout

My mother was diagnosed with cancer December 13, 2005. She is incredibly brave, and we have every reason to hope for a full recovery. In the meantime, I hope that she knows how many people love and admire her. I realized, while looking at pictures from earlier in the year, she had been sick for a long time and that nothing had changed. Cancer may have changed her life, but it did not change her. She is still a mother, daughter, sister, friend, businesswoman, an avid reader and a quilter. She is still my mom.

ALISON FLYNN

★ Paris, France

TOP SECRET
TOP SECRET

WHO COULD

TOP SECRET
TOP SECRET
TOP SECRET
TOP SECRET
TOP SECRET
TOP SECRET
TOP SECRET

NOTHING to gain...
i'm hollow + ALONE.

the way everyone is looking at me...

Give i top feel... have but NEGATIVITY? i can't trust no one by

REJECTED

have known?

· that this girl made cuts in her skin every night in a desperate attempt just to feel?
· that she threw up after every meal just trying to be beautiful?
· that this girl would hate herself so much that she would stash pills "just in case"?
· that this girl felt this way at only 16 years old?

· that sometimes that girl is still ME now.

CONFIDENTIAL   CONFIDENTIAL   CONFIDENTIAL   CONFIDENTIAL

WHO COULD HAVE KNOWN?

SUPPLIES:
Patterned paper (BasicGrey); textured cardstock (Bazzill); chipboard letters (BasicGrey, Heidi Swapp); phrase stamp (7gypsies); distress ink (Ranger); pen

JOURNALING

Who could have known...

That this girl made cuts in her skin every night in a desperate attempt just to feel?

That she threw up after every meal just trying to be beautiful?

That this girl would hate herself so much that she would stash pills "just in case"?

That this girl felt this way at only 16 years old?

That sometimes that girl is still me now.

The Story Behind the Layout

I created this layout after coming across this picture of me when I was in high school. What struck me first was how happy and put together I was. A part of me wanted to scrapbook the happy page that detailed the surface stuff that I had going on at that time (homework, friends, dances, etc.). But I couldn't deny any longer a part of the reality that was in that—the girl who was in constant pain, constantly doubting and self-loathing. At that time I was slowly destroying myself and shut off from the world around me. My parents had divorced, and I thought I was the ugliest person to ever step foot on this earth. I felt that no matter how hard I tried the "right way" to change things, I would always fail. So I resorted to cutting myself and suffered from bulimia and depression. I hid these things well, but I know that truth and I know there are still times that I struggle with these same issues. My hope in sharing this page is that maybe others will realize that they are not alone.

RACHEL HALL

★ Prescott, Arizona

I was born and raised in the small town of Prescott, Arizona, and reside there to this day. I married my husband when I was seventeen years old, and we have been married for seven years, and have one daughter, Roslyn. I'm a stay-at-home mom and work part-time at our local scrapbook store designing and teaching classes. My passions include scrapbooking, history, art, writing, photography and raising my family. My aim is to one day have a history degree, with an emphasis in women's studies. I am constantly seeing beauty in the world around me. My goal is to share this beauty with others, mainly my daughter.

Surviving BuLImIa

In the end, the only one I blame is myself. I wanted to be thin - supermodel ballerina thin.

No hips, just bones. I was scared of fat. I obsessively logged food from age 10 →

but it wasn't until junior high that I learned about how to "eat" and not eat. I hid my secret until my late 20s - although sometimes I would get "caught" purging - or my binge stash discovered.

In the end, however, only I could stop the cycle.

THIS IS NOT FAT

SURVIVING BULIMIA

SUPPLIES:
Textured cardstock (Bazzill); acrylic paint, rub-on letters, letter stickers (Making Memories); stamp (Ken Brown Stamps); chipboard letters (Li'l Davis Designs); solvent ink (Tsukineko); pens (American Crafts, Sanford Corp.)

JOURNALING

In the end, the only one I blame is myself. I wanted to be thin—supermodel ballerina thin. No hips, just bones. I was scared of fat. I obsessively logged food from age 10, but it wasn't until junior high that I learned about how to "eat" and not eat. I hid my secret until my late 20s—although sometimes I would get "caught" purging or my binge stash discovered. In the end, however, only I could stop the cycle.

The Story Behind the Layout

This layout is really different from any piece of art I've created. I've never been very "open" about my bulimia (dirty little secret and all that), but I guess you could say I'm really putting it out in the open here. This was a cathartic piece of art as it has helped me get through one of the steps of recovery from something that has plagued me for most of my life—an unhealthy relationship with food. This photo was actually used in another layout I did for the Memory Makers book *Totally Teen*, and I kept looking at it in my galleries and wondering why I've spent my entire life feeling like I was fat—even when I clearly wasn't. This layout itself came pouring out of me in less than thirty minutes. I was almost too frightened to submit it, but I figured once I hit the send button, I would truly be free of my secret. And there it went. And here it is. I feel better already!

JENNIFER LYNN MOODY

★ Lewisville, Texas

I'm a thirty-something single business owner living in the Dallas suburbs. I travel over two-hundred thousand miles a year—both for work and to see my boyfriend, who lives half a continent away! When I'm not traveling, I enjoy food out with my friends and creating art. I've been scrapbooking ever since (sometimes too much!), hanging I could pick up a glue stick. I'm the co-author of *Self-Centered* and have been featured in several other scrapbooking publications.

Just over that bridge, I can hear my former life calling out to me. That life filled with lights, late nights, dancing, and raw freedom. A life where watches didn't matter because time didn't exist... the future was mine for the taking. That was over five years ago and so much has changed. My body now a shadow of itself, ravaged by illness, sits on the opposite side of the bridge and longs to see the lights.

beyond the bridge

BEYOND THE BRIDGE

SUPPLIES:
Patterned papers (American Crafts, Urban Lily); textured cardstock (Bazzill); chipboard letters (Li'l Davis Designs); letter stickers (BasicGrey); decorative brads (Making Memories); acrylic stars (Heidi Swapp); pens (EK Success, Sanford Corp.); embroidery thread

The Story Behind the Layout

As you are growing up, you never really believe that anything bad can happen to you. I remember worrying that one day I would get sick, unable to care for myself, but those were just thoughts that would float in and out of my mind. As I reached my mid-twenties, those fleeting thoughts began to become grounded in reality. At that time, I was working hard and having fun in the fabulous city of New York. I crossed those New York bridges as if I owned them. They were my "bridges to freedom" that connected me to inspiring artwork, culture, music and friends. Those were some of the best days of my life.

The stress of work and life took its toll on an underlying health condition I had dealt with since adolescence. Without warning, those carefree days and nights were all but gone. They were replaced by pain and worry, some of the worst days of my life. Those same bridges were now impassable to me. I began to hate them, even fear their possible frailty. It hurt to realize that the best part of my life was possibly over.

Now, five years later, my health has greatly improved. I have forced myself to look back at those New York bridges and cross them again. Although I may not be crossing into the life I once led, I still enjoy the experiences I have today. I will never loose that ache in my heart to return to those days of lights and music. But I also know that the best days of my life lie ahead as I watch my daughter enjoy the lights and music for herself.

JOURNALING

Just over that bridge, I can hear my former life calling out to me. That life filled with lights, late nights and raw freedom. A life where watches didn't matter because time didn't exist...the future was mine for the taking. That was over five years ago and so much has changed. My body now a shadow of itself, ravaged by illness, sits on the opposite side of the bridge and longs to see the lights.

ALEXIS HARDY

★ Franklin Square, New York

I reside in the fabulous state of New York, with my husband of five years and our beautiful daughter. After working in the field of education for five years, I decided to become a stay-at-home mom so I could teach my daughter and watch her grow.

I live my life seeing art in every-day moments. From my daughter's smile, to the silhouette of a bare tree against a winter sky, art surrounds us all the time. I photograph nearly everything that inspires me: anything that makes me smile, cry or feel that rhythm deep within my soul. But photographs can only say so much. I started scrapbooking so I could express the profound effect that each of those captured moments had on me. Through paper and ink, thread and metal, I create layouts that bring the emotion and excitement of my photographs to life.

{ 71 }

Always from place to place my head needs to rest

Siem Reap '02

ALWAYS FROM PLACE TO PLACE

SUPPLIES:
Textured cardstock (Bazzill); rub-on letters, foam alphabet stamps, stitched tile (Making Memories); page pebble map (Jest Charming); wire; pen; staples; sandpaper

The Story Behind the Layout

For as long as I can remember, I've wanted to travel. When I was a teenager, my legs started to become extremely restless. My parents gave me permission to go as soon as I turned 18, so exactly two weeks after that birthday I was on a plane going places! The best part of traveling to me is meeting the most interesting and intriguing people and seeing all the amazing places. It really made me appreciate the small things in life.

There was a downside though. After about seven years of continuously moving around, I discovered I couldn't stay in any one place for more than a few months without feeling the need to move. I found I wasn't able to build relationships or friendships any longer because both they and I knew I was going to pack up and leave again. Now that I have settled down a bit and have a family of my own, I really feel I need to rest my head and feel at home.

VIVIAN BONDER

★ Darlington, Australia

I believe I was born to create! As long as I can remember, I've been creating things, whether painting, photography or writing. When traveling, I always carry a journal with me to include the important things I see. A friend introduced me to scrapbooking in 2002 and the journey has gone fast from there. I am a regular contributor to the Dutch *Creatief met Foto's* and have made quite a few canvases for them. I will be published in *Scrapbook Creations* in 2006, and have done several albums, as well as other items for clients. I've always tried to bring my own personality into everything I do.

P.S. BREATHE

SUPPLIES:
Cardstock (Paper Company); pre-printed transparency (K&Company); rub-on letters (7gypsies); chipboard letters (Li'l Davis Designs); chipboard heart (Heidi Swapp); safety pins (Making Memories); distress ink (Ranger); tag (from a pair of jeans)

The Story Behind the Layout

The premise of my layout simply states the condition I was in after resigning from my full-time position. I found it very cathartic to simply put my thoughts down on paper that day so I could press on. Although it has been tough, and I know it will be tougher before it gets better, I do believe it was in my best interest. Things such as this are never easy yet make us better people in the long run!

JOURNALING

The sun was shining that day! Or was it gloomy? Perhaps it was my mood or the challenges I was faced with up to this point! It is never easy to resign from a job! A safe haven if you will? Where was I going! Why was I unprepared! How would I support my family? How would I support my well-being? All I knew for sure is that it would be a new beginning! Am I scared? You better believe I am! Will it be an easy process? Absolutely not! The one thing I know to be true...I am ready to keep growing, to evolve and to enjoy the process! Let it begin...

RACHEL CARLSON

★ Highlands Ranch, Colorado

Still on vacation in Colorado or so it seems—ha! Moved from Austin, Texas, in 2002—yes, for the mountains! My love for paper arts and photography was discovered many moons ago! I'm at my best when I'm playing with paper, running with scissors or holding a camera. Recently, I was reunited with my scrapbook from eighth grade—eek! What was I thinking? Tape went a long way back in the day! Luckily I found the best way to create art and document moments the safe way in 2004, and have been enjoying it ever since! I've had the pleasure of being on a few design teams and am currently on a Canadian team for my second contract. I'm very lucky to have a local group that I create art with (hugs to the scrap-scrap sisterhood!). It's a good thing that the loves of my life, Rich, Amber and our furry-girl, LoMein, put up with me!

FRAGILE

URGENT

ADDICTION

Dependence

Am I doomed to be a smoker for the rest of my life? Am I to spend the rest of my days huddled outside in the cold with the other smokers? Will I continue to be looked down upon by non-smokers? It isn't easy being a smoker in this day and age. I started smoking when I was 13. It was cool! I didn't inhale at first, just sucked in the smoke and blew it out. Peer pressure can be such a cruel thing. Wanting to be cool and do grown up things gave me the incentive to keep on puffing till I got it right and it wasn't long before I became thoroughly addicted.

35 years have passed and I think about quitting everyday. Even tried it a couple of times. I'm normally such a strong person. I've never been weak, but yet this addiction has such a strong hold of me. I will never forget the first time I tried to quit. It was after my father had open-heart surgery. The image of what I saw when I was allowed to go see him for the first time will forever be burned in my mind. What I saw brought tears to my eyes and it literally broke my heart. Dad looked like death. His color did not look natural. His body was all puffed and swelled up. He had tubes sticking out everywhere and he was hooked up to many machines. The thing that scared me the most was the respirator that was helping him breath. You could hear the machine filling his lungs with life. Seeing dad laying there in this condition, personally brought it home to me, how fragile life can be. How precious it is. How much I would miss my dad if he weren't here. I knew right at that very moment that I better quit my own Smoking habit before it happens to me. I thought how could I put my kids through the hell seeing me laying there helpless, near death and hooked up to scary sounding machines? Seeing this would make anyone quit right? Not me.

Nor did I quit the second or third time of trying, although the third time I quit for a month, which was the longest I'd ever gone. I constantly punish myself for giving in to my addiction after being smoke free for so long. I remember my hands trembling as I drove to the gas station to buy cigarettes. When I lit up that cigarette after 32 smoke free days, I immediately felt a gush of relief. It felt so good to inhale that cigarette smoke and feel the nicotine do its evil work. I felt good knowing that my depression was lifting. I also felt a bit dizzy, like that first time I inhaled a cigarette. I failed again. I'm ashamed having to admit my lack of will power, my defeat, and my human weakness. I will try again...and I will keep on trying. For my kids, and my grandkids, I will face this addiction head on, I will fight...and I will win.

STRONG

time

ADDICTION

SUPPLIES:
Patterned paper (BasicGrey); pre-printed transparency (Creative Imaginations); chipboard letters (Li'l Davis Designs); clock face (7gypsies); decorative brads (Making Memories); page pebble (Junkitz); vellum; transparency

The Story Behind the Layout

I have never created a layout for a specific call before, but when this particular call came out, I knew I had the right subject matter. This layout was difficult for me to do because it forced me to face my issues head on. I had to admit the fact that I'm still a smoker, I'm weak and I lack willpower. Creating this page helped me face the fact that I really need to quit. It helped me understand that I can't quit because my family wants me to…I have to quit for me and, more importantly, for my health. I want to watch my grandsons grow up. I want to continue photographing them and I want to create memories. So for now, I'll continue fighting my addiction. And with the help of scrapbooking, and keeping my hands busy, I'm going to win!

CHERYL BAASE

★ Lansing, Michigan

I live in Michigan with my husband, Mike, and our menagerie of rescued animals. I am a mother to three grown children and grandmother to six beautiful grandsons, whom are all the inspiration for my photos and scrapbook pages. I've been scrapbooking for about five years, but have become serious about it over the last year. I enjoy trying new things and have a huge love of ink. I ink everything! My life is very busy…running a household, working a full-time job and doing animal rescue, but I find that scrapbooking is my outlet.

true confessions story
A LONG TIME AGO

the juicy part

HELLO my name is LanA

HELLO MY NAME IS LANA

SUPPLIES:
Patterned papers (7gypsies, Autumn Leaves, Bo-Bunny Press); ribbon (Prima); letter stickers, hinges, gems, brads (Making Memories); rub-ons (7gypsies, Autumn Leaves); paper flowers (Prima); other ribbon

JOURNALING

Hello, my name is Lana and I have a story. Two stories really. My life before I quit drugs and alcohol and my life after. The story up until four and a half years ago goes like this: Scared child, alcoholic family, abuse, no focus, teen angst, trouble, drugs, escape from reality, bliss, quit athletics, quit school, careless living, isolation, depression, more drinking and drugs, insane lifestyle, insane behavior, chaos, unmanageable life, out of control, descending faster, plummeting, crashing and landing in rehab. Story 2 appears in the far distance. It took a couple years of trial and error, hitting my head against the wall over and over before finally giving up. Letting go. Surrendering. I accepted I could no longer do this anymore. I just can't drink like others. I can't stop like others. I don't stop until I've lost everything. But what a surprise to learn that I was giving up that misery in exchange for happiness and peace I NEVER believed existed. The second story goes like this: Hopeful but struggling, recovering, learning, began loving myself, struggled less, my first daughter was born, lived some adventures, found pride in my work, started loving life for the first time, met my match, married him, lived some more adventures, had baby #2, continued recovering, continued learning, found true friends, found true contentment. I try daily to recover and grow. I can as long as I don't drink.

The Story Behind the Layout

Creating this layout was in many ways a no-brainer. I know who I am and recognize what I am to be grateful for. As explained in the journaling, I have a very different past life than what I live now. I am not the same person I was. In this layout, the self-portrait is a metaphor, to say that there is more than meets the eye. The staged photo of my coffee cup and jacket comfy in their places around a table is to symbolize how I made the changes that I did. I made changes with the help of others. It was and still is simply a group of people gathering and sharing about their own experience, strength and hope. And yes, we often chat over coffee. They help me see the light, so to speak. They help me remain honest, open and willing. And the biggest one is that they understand me. I can't stay sober without the help of others. And I can't have anything great in life without staying sober. So really, I owe them my life. In the spirit of my adventurous past and wandering ways, I used 7gypsies paper in my background design. The sprinkling of flowers, gems, and brads is to reflect the miracle that happened in my life. It is a miracle that I am alive, sober and happy. And I pay it forward by being myself and sharing my story.

LANA RAPPETTE

★ Benton Harbor, Michigan

I stumbled into scrapbooking, as we know it now, in March 2005 when I quit my technical corporate job to stay home with our comedian daughter, Lucy, and prepare for our second child, Ruby, who was born in May. Scrapbooking fits me to a T. I have always used journals, photos, paintings, drawings and other art to express the "here and now" of my life. I credit much of my inspiration to my husband, Mike, who has given me two children, a happy marriage, many laughs and plenty of Michigan adventures. These memories are the true treasures that deserve every glue dot, rubber stamp and inked edge in which I use to document it all.

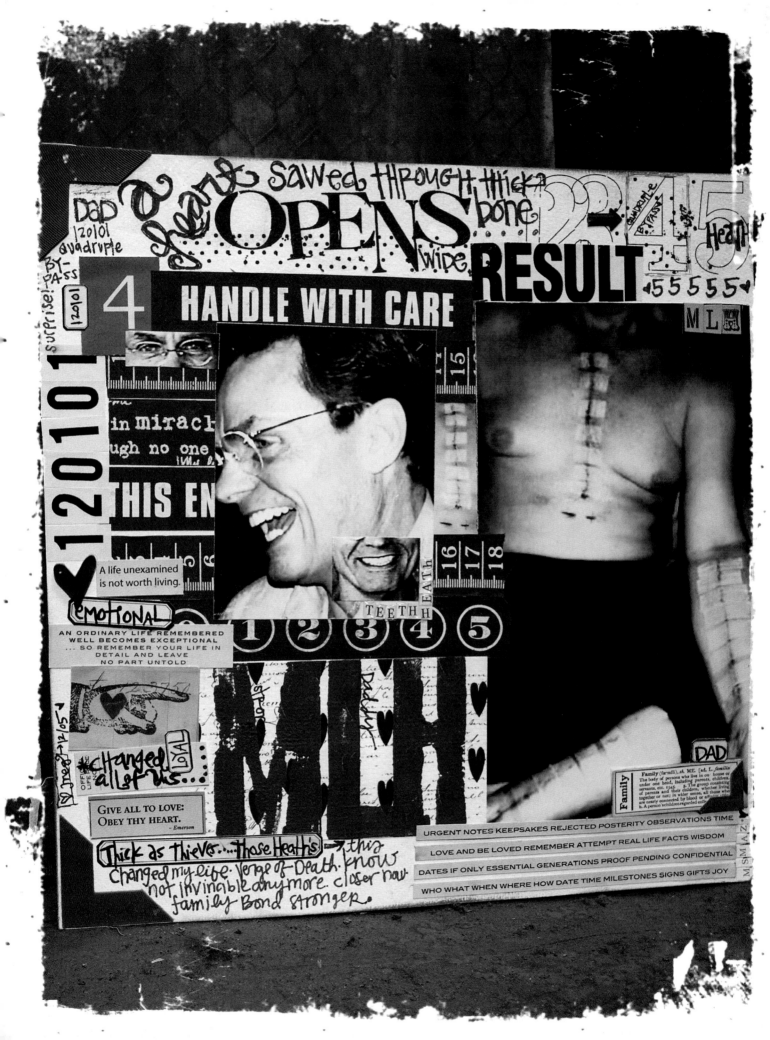

Heart sawed through thick bone

OPENS wide

DAD
12010l
quadruple
BY-PASS

surprise! 12010l

120101

4

HANDLE WITH CARE

RESULT

QUADRUPLE BY-PASS

Heart

5 5 5 5 5

ML

in mirach
ugh no one

THIS EN

A life unexamined
is not worth living.

EMOTIONAL

AN ORDINARY LIFE REMEMBERED
WELL BECOMES EXCEPTIONAL
... SO REMEMBER YOUR LIFE IN
DETAIL AND LEAVE
NO PART UNTOLD

TEETH

① ② ③ ④ ⑤

changed
all of this...

LOYAL

GIVE ALL TO LOVE:
OBEY THY HEART.
— Emerson

MLH

DAD

Family   Family (fa-mill), sb. ME. [ad. L. familia
The body of persons who live in on house o
under one head, including parents, children,
servants, etc. 1545.   2. The group consti-
of parents and their children, whether living
together or not; in wider sense, all those who
are nearly connected by blood or of those who
b. A person's children regarded colle

URGENT NOTES KEEPSAKES REJECTED POSTERITY OBSERVATIONS TIME

LOVE AND BE LOVED REMEMBER ATTEMPT REAL LIFE FACTS WISDOM

DATES IF ONLY ESSENTIAL GENERATIONS PROOF PENDING CONFIDENTIAL

WHO WHAT WHEN WHERE HOW DATE TIME MILESTONES SIGNS GIFTS JOY

Thick as thieves....those Heath's → this
changed my life. Verge of Death. know
not invincible anymore. closer now
family Bond stronger.

A HEART OPENS

SUPPLIES:
Textured cardstock (Bazzill); gaffer tape, stickers, arrow (7gypsies); epoxy letter stickers (K&Company); tab stickers (Li'l Davis Designs); foam alphabet stamps, rub-on letters (Making Memories); photo corners (Scrapworks); "Result" sticker (Wal-Mart)

The Story Behind the Layout

On December first of 2001, my slender, fifty-one-year-old dad was walking downtown on a break from work. He started to have chest pains, and thought to himself, "Wow, getting old is rough," but continued on with his day. The same night, the pains returned while he was vacuuming the house. The next morning, my dad went to the doctor and had a stress test on his heart. He was told, "We will not sign to have you released from this hospital until you have surgery." There were major blockages in the arteries of my dad's heart. The next day my dad had a quadruple bypass.

This event shocked my family. My parents have been together for thirty-seven years, and I don't know of an event that has changed my mom more than this surgery. The night before the surgery, I don't think she slept more than three hours. The morning of the surgery she arrived at the hospital around 4 a.m. and sat outside my dad's room, waiting until he woke up. I think it was her way of protecting him.

I saw my dad immediately following surgery in the recovery ICU. He was writhing around fighting the anesthesia and he looked like he was dead. I walked in the room and saw him and turned around and walked right back out crying. I have never forgotten that moment; it was then I realized our lives are fragile and my dad is not invincible.

Today, thanks to the surgery and daily exercise, my dad has fully recovered and is healthier than ever.

MEGHAN
HEATH-DYMOCK

★ Gilbert, Arizona

My scrapbooks are my journals. I moved from Utah to Arizona a year ago so my husband, Tyson, could pursue his MBA. I talk daily to my sister, Aubrie, miss my family in Utah, walk into my studio just for the delicious smell of scrapbook supplies, laugh with Tyson and visit Starbucks for iced white soy mochas.

MY MOMENTS OF...

SUPPLIES:
Patterned papers (BasicGrey, Die Cuts With A View); cardstock, vellum quote (Die Cuts With A View); tags (BasicGrey); decorative brads, paper flowers, velvet trim, rub-on words (Making Memories); hinge, mini brads (Daisy D's); letter stickers (Creative Imaginations); rub-ons (Déjà Views)

JOURNALING

Cancer...six letters...one word... Moments of...indescribable fear! Am I going to die? Then... moments of amazing courage... I will live and I will fight this disease! Many moments of heartfelt hope for a wonderful future. All moments of self discovery.

The Story Behind the Layout

I created this layout as a way of recognizing a very challenging time in my life. I was diagnosed with breast cancer in April, 2005. It was, without hesitation, the most frightening thing I've ever experienced.

Facing my mortality was not something I expected to have to think about at thirty-five. Realizing we don't always have the option of choosing our life experiences, I decided that I could not dwell on the negative aspects of my situation. This began my journey of true self-discovery. The substance of my life came into clear focus in the months following my diagnosis when my treatments became increasingly more draining on my body and spirit.

It was not until my basic foundation had been rocked so completely that I was able to redefine my purpose in life. I was forced to face life in very realistic terms. I looked deeply into my soul and decided to live life with an intensity I had never before understood. I decided that I could not live the rest of my life worrying about what could happen; instead I would cherish every moment and live each day to the fullest.

Months later, I am a deeply changed woman. I am healing. I feel emotionally stronger than I have ever been. I can now reflect and feel proud of the way I ultimately handled my diagnosis and treatment. I am thankful for the wonderful support of my family, friends and the cancer community. I am truly blessed to be a Breast Cancer Survivor.

DANA
HOLLIS MIRON

★ Farmington, Minnesota

I live with my husband, Scott, and my son, Kristofer. I've been scrapbooking for about three years and I am a self-confessed scrapbook supply shopaholic. I enjoy paper crafts, card making, sewing, reading and nature photography excursions with my husband.

4 • 05 • 2003

Dear Connor,
Sitting there, holding a day old Baby Olivia. I had a knowing feeling A sense that a little life was building inside of me. But after three heartbreaking miscarriages. I didn't say a word... content with just the possibility of a baby. This was the beginning of becoming your MOM

The Day I Knew....

THE DAY I KNEW

SUPPLIES:
Patterned papers (BasicGrey); letter stamps
(PSX Design); brads (SEI): paper flowers
(Prima); stamping ink

The Story Behind the Layout

After three miscarriages, I had just about given up on having a baby of my own. I had told myself that with my next pregnancy, I wouldn't get my hopes up. Then my good friend, Aysu, had her baby, Olivia. I went to see her in the hospital the next day, and as I was holding that little day-old bundle, my mind started running. Doing the math, counting the days. "Wait!" I thought. "I could be pregnant...right now." So I smiled for the camera, content with little Olivia in my arms, and smiled. Smiled because I was holding a baby, smiled because I knew I had another chance at becoming a mom. I didn't take my pregnancy test until a week later. And it was positive. Eight months later, I was a mom for the very first time.

JOURNALING

Dear Connor,

Sitting there, holding a day-old baby Olivia, I had a knowing feeling. A sense that a little life was building inside of me. But after three heartbreaking miscarriages, I didn't say a word...content with just the possibility of a baby. This was the beginning of becoming your mom.

MISSY GLEASON

★ Galloway, Ohio

I am the oldest of three girls. I am a wife to a police officer. I am a mother to a rambunctious two-year-old boy. I am a television news producer. My life is crazy, noisy and draining...but I enjoy it. I'd like to have a lot more time with my family, and a little less stress. I found a wonderful outlet when I discovered scrapbooking. I was always the kid who sat with the family pictures, looked at every single one, and asked who everyone was in the photos. I love the stories behind the pictures, and with scrapping, I get to create little works of art that tells stories that will live long beyond my time on earth.

UNWRITTEN

Christina

i am unwritten... can't read my mind
i am undefined. i'm just beginning... the
pen is in my hand, ending unplanned. i'm
staring at the blank page before you... open
up a dirty window... let the sun illuminate
the words you cannot find. Speak the words on
your lips. Today is where your book begins...the rest
is still unwritten.

"FIND OUT WHO YOU ARE AND DO IT ON PURPOSE."
-DOLLY PARTON

PORTRAIT OF A WOMAN >>>

Every little girl dreams of being a woman...older, sophisticated and self sufficient. She dreams of a day when she can go off and live her own life the way she intends to. The transition is slow. It is a combination of time and experience that shapes her. Then, one day she wakes up and realizes the transition has happened...womanhood. She can't identify where or when it happened, it just did.

How do you define womanhood? Some think of womanhood as independence and strength, some think of womanhood as being feminine and demure, and some associate womanhood with a specific age or status. Each woman is unique. She is complex and yet simple in her needs. She is selfless, putting the needs of others before her own. She is sensitive and vulnerable, and yet strong enough to carry the weight of the world on her shoulders. She has a desire to care for others and to give of herself, even when there is nothing left to give.

UNWRITTEN

The Story Behind the Layout

While looking through pictures I had taken of myself, I was listening to "Unwritten," a song by Natasha Bedingfield. It was at that moment I realized that the wonderful song lyrics struck a cord with me. I'm just beginning my creative journey and the rest of it is still unwritten. I look pensive, unsure of the future and coupling the lyrics with this photo made a perfect combination.

SUPPLIES:
Patterned papers (Bo-Bunny Press, Imagination Project, me & my BIG Ideas); textured cardstock (Bazzill); acrylic flower, rub-on letters, decorative tape (Heidi Swapp); mailbox letter, lace, decorative brad (Making Memories); letter stickers (American Crafts, Chatterbox, Imagination Project, SEI); pens (American Crafts, Sakura of America); distress ink (Ranger); staples

CHRISTINA PADILLA

★ salinas, California

I'm a happy mother to my two-year-old son, Jaden Presley, and wife to my scrapbook-supportive husband, David. When I was a child, you could always find me with a coloring book and a big box of crayons. Even in my teens, I collected magazine clippings and school memorabilia, along with my own artwork and put it all together in albums. As an adult, I discovered the "acid-free" way of scrapbooking and never looked back! It now has become a way of life for me. I look at my daily life differently as a scrapbooker. Even ordinary days captured in a photo can become a lasting memory in a scrapbook page. I scrapbook whenever possible, I take tons of photos and I love every moment of it!

TIME of DAY

I read Somewhere that there are 2 IMPORTANT days in a person's life. The day they are born and the day they know WHY they are born. I'm not sure what day TIME I Know my purpose. Was it the DAY I get married or had my 1st child? Or was it the time that I understood that true living is living outside myself for others? There have been many DAYS and times that have been monumental in my life, so it would be hard to pin point which

1. I love the song by Steven Curtis Chapman "more to this life". In that song it says; there is MORE to this life than living & dying or even just trying to make it through the day. The message is simple but yet very profound. We each are given 24 hours in a day and we make choices every day for what we will do with them. TIME is a great opportunity. How can we use it to bless or minister to others? Are we a help OR a hindrance? I'm blessed to use my time on many things; my husband of 17 years, 4 children, aging parents, 5th grade girls Sunday school, neighbors friends and young moms that call for counsel. I feel STRETCH sometimes, but how blessed to be able to say that these are what give MORE to my life. I can't say what day I knew my PURPOSE, but I do know for these things & my Creator, for such a time as this I was placed upon the Earth.

From MORE TO THIS life by Steven Curtis Chapman

"But there's more to this life than living & dying, more than just trying to make it through the DAY; more to this life, MORE than these eyes alone can see, & there more than this life alone can be. Based on 1 Timothy 6:19

TIME OF DAY

SUPPLIES:
Patterned paper, clock sticker, large eyelet
(Creative Imaginations); textured cardstocks
(Bazzill, KI Memories); metal cross (EK Success);
concho (K&Company); chalk (Deluxe Designs);
rub-on letters, portobello (7 gypsies); distress ink
(Ranger); letter stickers (KI Memories); stamp
(Purple Onion Designs); pen (EK Success)

The Story Behind the Layout

I've done only a few pages about myself. I often put information like my favorite song or candy bar, and while I think those things are fun to mention, I wanted to go beyond that. This was the first time I had really poured my soul into journaling about myself. It was refreshing to get my thoughts out on paper. It's something I want my children to see and understand about their mom.

JOURNALING

I read somewhere that there are two important days in a person's life. The day they are born and the day they know why they are born. I'm not sure what day or time I knew my purpose. There have been many days that have been monumental in my life, so it would be hard to pin point which one.

I love the song by Steven Curtis Chapman "More to this Life." It says there is more to this life than living and dying, or even just trying to make it through the day. We each are given 24 hours in a day and we make choices for what we will do with them. How can we use it to bless or minister to others? I'm blessed to use my time on many things; my husband, four children, aging parents, 5th grade girls Sunday school, neighbors, friends and young moms that call for counsel. I feel stretched sometimes, but blessed to be able to say that these things are what give more to my life. I can't say what day I knew my purpose, but I do know for these things and my Creator, for such a time as this I was placed upon the earth.

KITTY FOSTER

★ Snellville, Georgia

I've been writing, designing and teaching in the scrapbooking field since 2000. I have been fortunate to be published in many scrapbook magazines and idea books and to be featured in an ongoing article in *Scrapbooking and Beyond*. I have designed for several companies, and I am currently designing for Fancy Pants Designs and Creative Imaginations. When not scrapbooking, you can often find me taking photographs on the sideline of one of my kid's sporting events, wearing funky jeans or reading a book.

right here, right now
..........and i am just fine..........

a long road. a difficult path. But
I'm here. Comfortable in my
skin. a comfortable soul. In
touch with myself. a sound
mind. a mom. a wife. a woman.
right here. right now. and I'm ok.

RIGHT HERE, RIGHT NOW

SUPPLIES:
Patterned papers (Scenic Route Paper Co.); cardstock (DMD); acrylic heart, foam heart stamp (Heidi Swapp); transparency; acrylic paint; marker

JOURNALING

A long road. A difficult path. But I am here. Comfortable in my skin. A comfortable soul. In touch with myself. A sound mind. A mom. A wife. A woman. Right here. Right now. And I'm OK.

The Story Behind the Layout

I have seen my fair share of ups and downs...losing our home, nearly losing our youngest daughter, and receiving my youngest daughter's autism diagnosis. Fighting what seems (some days) to be a losing battle in a lawsuit. Facing depression and loss head-on and winning. This layout is about just that...coming to terms. Acceptance. Dealing. Coping. Winning the battle within. Realizing that while life isn't easy, it doesn't have to be crippling. Letting go of the negative and holding onto the positive. Most of all, being thankful for it all. Without the pain, there would be no growth.

JAMIE WARREN

★ Rentz, Georgia

I am the proud mom of two beautiful little girls and the wife of one supportive husband. Originally from Orlando, Florida, I now live in a very small town in Georgia.

I have always loved photography and creating. Being able to combine the two has been a dream come true! My love for photography started at a young age and became a passion of mine as a teenager. I was introduced to scrapbooking by a friend and from that moment I was hooked. For me, scrapbooking is a creative outlet. I am able to share my love for my children, my husband and photography through my pages.

"DEVELOP AN APPRECIATION FOR THE PRESENT MOMENT"...that's what the fortune cookie said. How often do you get real wisdom from a fortune cookie? Usually I end up getting the ones that say "You are a kind person". (gee, thanks.) or something that's lame until you add "in bed" to the end and then it's slightly amusing. But this fortune- well, advice. is. serious. And so meant for me. DO THIS NISA. So often I'm waiting for the next thing...antsy, excited, or just plugging away, wishing for a music montage to speed up the process...to get to the good part. But this. is. it. THIS IS THE GOOD PART. This is your life Nisa. This beautiful mess. This cluttered lil house full of papers and photos and messy dishes and so much love. This laying on the couch tangled up with Ben and watching bad TV, with our lil pup always in the middle. This hanging out in the sunroom, me scrapping, him building a model plane, a mobile, a jet engine (what?) This working and playing and talking and laughing and crying and sighing...this everyday. This present moment is the good part. Gotta live it up.

listen

live it up.

THIS PRESENT MOMENT

Develop an appreciation for the
present moment.
Lucky Numbers 10, 37, 5, 47, 2, 31

YOU ARE HERE 26   27   28   29   30

20   21   22   23   24

THIS PRESENT MOMENT

SUPPLIES:
Patterned papers (7 gypsies, BasicGrey, Camden Fair, EK Success, KI Memories, Mara-Mi, My Mind's Eye, Scenic Route Paper Co., Scrapworks); assorted embellishments (7 gypsies, Design Originals, KI Memories, Making Memories); foam alphabet stamps (Li'l Davis Designs); square punches (Marvy/Uchida); rub-on letters (7 gypsies, Making Memories); acrylic paint; pen

JOURNALING

"DEVELOP AN APPRECIATION FOR THE PRESENT MOMENT"... that's what the fortune cookie said. How often do you get real wisdom from a fortune cookie? Usually I end up getting the ones that say, "you are a kind person" (gee, thanks.), or something that's lame until you add "in bed" to the end and then it's slightly amusing. But this fortune—well, advice—is serious. And so meant for me. DO THIS NISA. So often I'm waiting for the next thing...antsy, excited, or just plugging away...to get to the good part. But this is it. THIS IS THE GOOD PART. This is your life Nisa. This beautiful mess. This cluttered lil house full of papers and photos and messy dishes and so much love. This laying on the couch tangled up with Ben and watching bad TV, with our lil pup always in the middle. This hanging out in the sunroom, me scrapping, and him building a model plane, a mobile, a jet engine (what?). This working and playing and talking and laughing and crying and sighing...this everyday. This present moment is the good part. Gotta live it up.

The Story Behind the Layout

Why did I feel the need to make this page? Because I wanted to remember the wisdom in that li'l cookie...because it's the everyday things that make up this life and make it so wonderful...because if I don't make art I go crazy. This whole "present moment" thing is something I've been thinking a lot about this year. This "being there"...I need to do more of that. I tend to be a worrier. I'm easily excitable, and often I find myself either worried or excited about "what's next," and so missing all of the now. The everyday. I need to slow down and look around. Enjoy this. This now. This everyday. This is one of the reasons I adore scrapbooking. Not scrapping the holidays, birthdays and vacations...but all the little things in between. The little things we tend to forget. The little things that make this life so amazing and fantastic and chaotic and real. The little things I want to remember.

NISA FIIN

★ St. Paul, Minnesota

I live in St. Paul with my dreamy fiancé, Ben, and our nudey pup, Hooper. Seriously, she has no fur. I started collecting scrapbooking stuff years ago, but only really started scrapping this past spring. Scrapbooking has changed my life. Honestly. It is such an amazing outlet for me...the photography, the writing, the remembering, the paper, the gluing and the mess. I have met some of the coolest people since I started this crazy thing. I am obsessed with patterned paper. I am an emotional roller coaster at times. I have an awesome family. I talk a lot. Even to strangers. If you got points in life for chatting it up with strangers, I would so be winning. I'm almost always wearing a hoodie. And drinking cranberry juice. I love photography...a good photo can make my week. I can't keep a plant alive to save my life. I have trouble sleeping. I'm actually writing this now because I can't sleep. It's 4:42 a.m.

I WILL TRY...

SUPPLIES:
*Patterned papers (KI Memories);
cardstocks (Bazzill, KI Memories);
letter stickers (American Crafts);
jewels (Heidi Swapp); "goals" sticker
(7 gypsies); chipboard circles
(Technique Tuesday)*

The Story Behind the Layout

I strive to achieve the simplest goals or intentions based on my everyday life. I am constantly pushing myself not to be as much of a perfectionist. However, I really don't want to spend the rest of my life sweating the small stuff. Life is too short for that. Ironically, my layout portrays the sarcastic side of who I am. Most of it is really nothing for me to sweat over. The rest? Well, I do need a reality check and realize that life goes on. I am learning that other people aren't going to change just for me. I just need to let things roll of my shoulders and worry about what is most important...the welfare of my family, our health and well-being. I do believe in change. If I didn't, I wouldn't try to change my own habits. In realizing this, I am getting more comfortable recognizing that I am not perfect. I am me, and I will achieve these simple goals in my life, in due time.

CINDY LIEBEL

★ Fredericksburg, Virginia

I am the wife to my best friend, Tim, for almost four years, a mother to a lovely, vivacious and energetic little man, Tyler, and a stepmother to our Italian greyhound, Sky.

I've been scrapping since August 2003 and heavily addicted, obviously. This art form fills me up with excitement, relaxation and sanity. I love to create mini books and anything that can be altered, as well as create fun scrapbook pages. Currently, I am a teacher and designer for a local scrapbook store, and I've recently had some of my artwork published in magazines. I also enjoy sewing, home décor, photography and a collection of music that drives my fuel to create.

I'm extremely honored and proud to be a part of several design teams. There is nothing like being surrounded by talented women, who share the same love and passion as I do. I'm truly looking forward to a wonderful adventure that's ahead!

I feel that now, with a full time job, bills and responsibilities, I am officially an adult. But what now, what does that mean? Does that mean I should move out, should I be married with kids already? If so, I am a little behind. Some days I don't feel like an adult, but I can't avoid the inevitable.

adulthood...
now
what?

ADULTHOOD... NOW WHAT?

SUPPLIES:
Cardstock (Bazzill); letter stickers (Chatterbox, Doodlebug Design, KI Memories, Making Memories); photo corners (Scenic Route Paper Co.); paper flowers (Prima); brad (SEI); acrylic paint

JOURNALING

I feel that now, with a full-time job, bills and responsibilities, I am officially an adult. But what now, what does that mean? Does that mean I should move out, should I be married with kids already? If so, I am a little behind. Some days I don't feel like an adult, but I can't avoid the inevitable.

The Story Behind the Layout

I created this layout right after I had started a new job. For me, that was the milestone that made me an adult. I had worked part-time when I was going to college, and I felt that was an excuse to live at home and rely on my parents. Now that I have a full-time job, I guess I consider myself an adult...now what? Should I move out right away, should I try to save money? What should I do? This layout documented all the questions I had, and actually still have. I gave the photo an altered look to emphasize the blurriness and confusion I was feeling. The dots on the cardstock were created with a pencil eraser and acrylic paint.

NICHOLE PEREIRA

★ Santa Clara, California

I am in my mid-twenties and pass the day working as a children's librarian. I don't have any children yet, but my favorite subjects are my goddaughter, my pets and my fiancé.

I have been scrapping for about six years, but only daily for the past two years and I am totally addicted! I love both the landscape and portrait orientations. My favorite supplies are cardstock, alphabet stickers, brads and cardstock! My favorite tools are my corner rounder, craft knife and anywhere hole punch.

I have always used scrapbooking as a way to capture memories. My scrapbooks aren't in chronological order, but each page and each picture holds a special memory or thought for me. It could be something as simple as a soda can or building, or something more meaningful like my family. Overall, scrapbooking has brought a new element to my life.

It's been a long while since I've been in a relationship, and although I've got other things to worry about, it's been on my mind a lot. Although I'm happy for them, I can't help but feel a little envious of my friends who are madly in love. I can't help but wonder if I'll end up as a washed-up old maid. I can't help but wonder if I'm not pretty enough. I'm sick of falling for guys who didn't feel the same way or have things not work out the way I wanted them to but I also won't just fall for anybody. I can only hope that he's around the corner. 12/05.

looking for love

Single & looking.

26, SAF, 5'0", 115, brown eyes, black-brn. hair

enjoys sports, photography, writing, eating, music

seeks attractive & caring SM, 19-22,

intelligent, like sports, non-smokers.

SINGLE & LOOKING

SUPPLIES:

Patterned paper (SEI); cardstock (DMD); stickers (KI Memories); heart (My Mind's Eye); rub-on letters (Scrapworks); ribbon (American Crafts); paper flowers (Prima); rhinestones (Darice); notebook paper

JOURNALING

It's been a long while since I've been in a relationship, and although I've got other things to worry about, it's been on my mind a lot. Although I'm happy for them, I can't help but feel a little envious of my friends who are madly in love. I can't help but wonder if I'll end up as a washed-up old maid. I can't help but wonder if I'm not pretty enough. I'm sick of falling for guys who didn't feel the same way or have things not work out the way I wanted them to. But I also won't just fall for anybody. I can only hope that he's around the corner.

20, SWF, 5'0", 115, brown eyes, black-brn. hair, enjoys sports, photography, writing, eating, music. Seeks attractive and caring SM, 19-22, intelligent, like sports, non-smoker.

The Story Behind the Layout

When I look around me, it seems as if everyone has a significant other. I seem to be one of the only single ones. Sometimes, it is frustrating. Of course, I'm happy for those who are happily attached, but at the same time, I'm jealous. As much as I want my own significant other, I refuse to compromise my standards until I find a guy that is the perfect fit for me.

CAROLINE IKEJI

★ Alhambra, California

As a child, I loved stickers and stationery products, so it is no surprise that years later, I picked up scrapbooking as my hobby and creative passion. I completed my first scrapbook in eighth grade as a homework project following a trip to Washington, D.C. After dabbling in scrapbooking for a couple of years, I became hooked in January 2005, and never looked back.

When I am not scrapping, I am busy completing my third year at a local community college. I plan to pursue journalism, and I am currently working as the managing editor for the campus newspaper. I enjoy shopping, eating, reading magazines, collecting lip gloss, listening to music and spending time with loved ones.

Tumbleweed

It's November. Another year almost done. When I look back on the past year, the person who stands out most in my mind is mum. How our relationship has grown and changed. How she has grown and changed before this year, she decided on her own to change and to example her role in relationships in her life. I was so happy. No matter what the years following her retirement held in store for her or have been filled with, she is happy. Her face, it's a doubedeedle, genuine, full, real smile. She is a different person for the better. Just look at the youth, ambition, understanding — and lessons learned. Took that one moment, and probably more... and was happy. The voice of support. The voice of reason. The voice of my mum. ...k. I wasn't there just mum and dad, but I've heard the story all over. She went chasing that tumbleweed... and caught it. And yet — it's there now. I can see it come alive when she plays with jaxon, or when she's talking about new ideas and plans she wants to... tative of this woman.

There's a story about a road trip up to hat creek, on the highway in the white truck. Spirit and spontaneity has not often present when we were growing up.

i love the tale of the tumbleweed. it is so repres...

somewhat free. somewhat tangled... the si... gnature windswept curls.

TALE OF THE TUMBLEWEED

SUPPLIES:
Patterned papers (7 gypsies, Chatterbox, Making Memories); textured cardstock (Bazzill); solvent ink (Tsukineko); pen

JOURNALING

It's November. Another year almost done. When I look back on the past year, the person who sticks out most in my mind is mum. How our relationship has grown and changed. How she has grown and changed. She decided on her own to change her role in the relationships in her life. I was so happy when she made the choice to retire. No matter what the years following her retirement held in store for her, she is a different person for the better. Just look at her face. It's a gorgeous, genuine, real smile. She took that one moment, and probably more... and was happy. She is a role model. The voice of reason. The voice of support. The voice of my mum.

There's a story about a road trip up to Hat Creek. Mum spotted a tumbleweed rolling down the road. Urging dad to pull over, she went chasing that tumbleweed...and caught it. That spirit and spontaneity was not often present when we were growing up. And yet—it's there now. I can see it come alive when she plays with Jaxon, or when she's talking about new ideas and plans. I love the Tale of the Tumbleweed. It is so representative of this woman. Somewhat free. Somewhat tangled...the signature windswept curls.

The Story Behind the Layout

My relationship with my mother has become better and better over the last several years. Ever since the tumbleweed event took place, I look at that tumbleweed hanging on the wall in my parents' house and imagine her chasing it down the highway. It has always appealed to me as a piece of art, but now that she and I are closer than ever, it appeals to me as a symbol of her spirit as well. I wanted to record that memory and always have it. Life was not always like it is now, and won't be in the future what it is now. Seemingly insignificant stories or events should always be remembered, right along with the major things we experience in life.

GENEVIEVE SIMMONDS

★ Vancouver, Canada

Art has always been a passion for me. Since I can remember, I have loved to draw and paint. I learned different techniques and obtained new skills throughout school...but no matter what, art has always been in my life in some form or another. When I found scrapbooking in February of 2005, it just stuck. It feels so natural to mix photography with art and writing... leaving behind a family legacy and providing myself with a creative outlet at the same time. I often refer to scrapbooking as my therapy; I swear it helps keep me sane and grounded. It provides an opportunity to express any emotion, and I really do try to scrap openly and honestly about all the times in my life—good and bad.

I live in Vancouver, British Columbia, with my husband of almost three years and my four-year-old son. The city of Vancouver and surrounding areas (mountains, beaches and islands) provide so much inspiration. I currently work in graphics for an optical disc manufacturing business. Sometimes I let my "designer's eye" lead me and sometimes I tell it to take a hike and I throw all the rules out the window. There is just so much to be had from experiencing life as an artist.

b & w

Life is not always Black & White... Not until my 30's did I begin to realise that life is not as simple as being black or white. Once I discovered this, life became more complex but also more interesting.

I have realised that people including myself are complicated, that our thoughts and views evolve as our lives change, and that is O.K. Since this realisation, I have learnt more about myself in the last few years than I had ever known. With this new found open mind, I am looking forward to discovering more about myself and more about the people and the world around me.

BLACK & WHITE

SUPPLIES:

Textured cardstock, letter sticker (Doodlebug Design); chipboard letters (Heidi Swapp); ribbon (American Crafts); paper flowers (Prima); gel pen

The Story Behind the Layout

I know it sounds cliché, but turning thirty was like having a light switched on in my head. I have made so many discoveries about myself since reaching this milestone. I have become more confident within myself, I worry less what other people think, and I have become more honest with myself. I am not naïve enough anymore to think that this is it. How I feel now about things is not necessarily how I will feel about them when I am forty, so I try to view people, life and its events with an open mind.

JUANITA WALKER

★ Queensland, Australia

While thinking about my biography I started thinking about the what, where and why, and I decided that my life is way too ordinary to go into all those details, so apart from some basic facts like...I am a woman, a wife of twelve years and a mother to three very gorgeous children. A design team member for an Aussie magazine and an Inspiration Team member for an Aussie online scrapbook store.

Instead, I decided I would share just what this crazy world of scrapbooking has given me. It has allowed me a creative outlet, an opportunity to generate something that is worthwhile; it has taken me on a journey that allow me to search my soul; it has made me think outside the square, and has taken me outside of my comfort zone. Scrapbooking has encouraged me to take chances...it has challenged me to put myself on the line and has helped me realize I can achieve my goals.

While creating my own work and enjoying the work of others, I have experienced a lot of emotion, occasionally anger and bitterness, sometimes tears, but most often laughter and joy.

For me, scrapbooking is not just a paper craft, it is not just a legacy for my children...it is so much more than that. It has been a vital tool in helping me develop and grow; it has allowed me to get to know myself in a more honest and true way.

ThIS is all I have

to proove that You existed. You were only mine for 7 days. Seven days of happiness, queasiness, fatigue & hunger. And then You Were gone. I never got to feel You kick, feel the pains of labor, or hold You. I am Angry. Why did this happen? Did I somehow cause this? So many questions. No answers. I am So Sad. I think of all the things I will not get to do with you... hold you, hug you, talk to you, watch you grow. But I know my Sadness will diminish. I know I will be Stronger because of You. I will cherish Your sisters even more. I will be thankful for all that I do have. Thank You little one, I will never forget You.

DATE: 11/11/2005 ——o DATE: 11/18/2005

LOVE LOST >>>

The experience of loss is not something one can explain. Sadly, the only way to understand it completely is to have been there and felt it yourself. Once you have experienced loss, you are never quite the same. For those left behind, there is pain, tears, heartache and questions. We often ask ourselves why, and yet, there is no good answer. It creates a void that can never be filled, and that person can never be replaced.

The death of our loved ones is inevitable. Some are expected and some take us by complete surprise. We can never fully prepare ourselves, and yet, we know in our mind that it can happen...but it happens when we least expect it. Some live long fulfilling lives and some are brief. Either way, they served their purpose in our lives and on this earth. And for a lifetime, we are forever changed.

STACEY
GEORGE

★ Pleasant Hill, Iowa

THIS IS ALL I HAVE

The Story Behind the Layout

SUPPLIES:
Patterned paper (Junkitz); textured cardstock (Bazzill); letter stickers (Making Memories); ribbon (Making Memories, Offray); date label (7 gypsies); acrylic heart (Heidi Swapp); distress ink (Ranger)

This layout was created after a miscarriage I had this past fall. When you have had two very easy, normal, healthy pregnancies, it is difficult to imagine that any other pregnancy might not end the same way. But now, after suffering two miscarriages since the birth of my second daughter, all of that has changed. This second miscarriage was very difficult for me. It made me feel very vulnerable, very alone. It made me question everything that happened during that short period of time. Did I cause this to happen? Did I exercise too much? Did I sleep too little? Get too stressed? Is there something wrong with me? And of course thoughts of the possibility that I may never be able to have more children weighed heavily on my mind. This layout was a documentation of all of those thoughts and feelings, as well as what I hope to learn and gain from this experience.

The guilt of a grieving mom is a pain no one should know.

Long after the pain has subsided, the survivor guilt still carries on.

Your heart aches, maybe you could have done more, maybe you could have saved him.

Maybe you could have skipped the trip that took your baby's life.

Maybe you could have changed it all.

Then one day you realize, yes, you could have changed it.

But you would have changed so much more.

You would have altered all of life's course, from people you met to lessons you learned.

You might not have the joy of other children in your life.

You might have never met your best friend.

You might not know how lucky you truly are, for those who have lost know how important little things are.

You might have saved him,

But today the guilt subsides somewhat.

You are thankful for the time you had, for the memories, the laughs, the lessons learned.

Today the guilt is less.

Today, you are truly a survivor.

- Dec. 2005 -

guilt

GUILT

SUPPLIES:
Patterned papers, chipboard letters
(BasicGrey); textured cardstock
(Bazzill); distress ink (Ranger)

The Story Behind the Layout

This is one of those layouts that I often do. I don't know where they are going, or where they will end; I just sit down and begin to type. Somewhere around the anniversary of one of my sons' deaths, I sat at the laptop and started my journaling. What I assumed was going to be a very heavy-hearted layout about the guilt I felt from the deaths of my children took a turn and stunned me.

I was no longer a guilty survivor. I was a mom who had done the best she could, a mom who had loved and lost, and yet I have gained so much. I was a mom who had finally come to terms with losing children. I found through the journaling that this would be my easiest Christmas in six years...I would hurt less and celebrate more. I would remember the good times, and forgive myself for the bad.

This layout was such an eye-opening experience to journal. Creating this page was such a growth experience for me...it will forever remain one of my most cherished layouts. I hope by sharing it, someone else out there may realize that they too are no longer a guilty survivor, but a survivor with many cherished memories and much to be thankful for.

JAMIE THARPE

★ Ozark, Alabama

I've always been a small town girl. My entire family lives in Alabama, so I chose to stay and raise my kids where I was raised. I have four children, Amos, Jakob, Savanna and Keenan. I'm also the mom to my two beautiful angels, Tyler and Hunter, who are forever gone from my life, but not my heart.

My children are the reason I scrapbook today. Through my efforts to create the perfect albums for each of them, I have learned so very much about myself.

I'm a loyal friend and confidant and I hold my memories dear because I learned young tomorrow doesn't always come. I hold my family and friends in my heart...after all, if you don't have them, you don't have anything.

broken

Jenni, Stacy & Melissa,
I Just WANT YOU ALL
TO KNOW EVERYTHING
IS Alright. The worst part
is over for me. It will take
A little while longer for
me to regain my strength —
so I can come home. I should
still be before your birthDAY
melissA, The Lord has really
blessed me, so much, I can't
wait to tell you. You can even
ask Aunt Dane + Uncle Bump how
much better I am doing. Now
that I'm feeling better, I
miss you girls more & more.

I Love you Jennifer with all my heart
I Love you Stacy with all my heart
I Love you melissa with all my heart
RememBer Mom + DAD will
Be home Real Soon. so DonT
worry about US. MAYBE you
GUYS CAN SHOW me how you
can Be mike Tyson
TAKE CARE ALL Three OV
you. Comfort one another
Be AT ALL TIMES. Be good to
Annette. thanK God for
ALL things.
              Love you
                    DAD

broken promises-
broken hearts-
and torn lives.
That's what you left
behind. You said you
were coming home and
everything was going
to be all right... I never
got to say goodbye. I
was only 13 when you
left me. I'm not sure
why God chose to take
the one thing in my life
that mattered most.
You see- when I lost
you- I lost myself. I lost
the will to do anything
in life. For a long time I
had to search for a
reason to live at all.

T O R N

IN MEMORY OF
BRUCE ROBERT BRENNAN
DATE OF BIRTH
October 31, 1956
DATE OF DEATH
January 27, 1989
PLACE OF SERVICES
Holy Resurrection
Orthodox Church
CLERGYMAN
V. Rev.
Gregory Rogers
PLACE OF INTERMENT
Calumet Park
Cemetery
ARRANGEMENTS BY

7535 Taft St. Merrillville, Indiana

BROKEN

SUPPLIES:
Patterned paper, typewriter letters (EK Success); acrylic letters (Heidi Swapp); acrylic paint, colored staples (Making Memories); cardstock, marker (Stampin' Up!); distress ink (Ranger); pen (American Crafts)

JOURNALING

Broken promises—broken hearts—and torn lives. That's what you left behind. You said you were coming home and everything was going to be alright...
I never got to say goodbye.
I was only 13 when you left me. I'm not sure why God chose to take the one thing in my life that mattered most. You see—when I lost you—I lost myself. I lost the will to do anything in life. For a long time I had to search for a reason to live at all.

The Story Behind the Layout

I was thirteen years old when I lost my father. It happened so quickly and so long ago that I can't remember all of the details. But I do remember the pain and heartbreak. After all, I was Daddy's little girl.

I will never forget the day he pulled me into my room to talk. We sat together as he explained as gently as he could that he was sick and had to go away for treatment. He asked me to help take care of my younger sisters. He promised that everything would be fine and that he would be home before I knew it.

I can't remember exactly how long he and my mother were gone. It was at least a month, maybe two. There were at least two surgeries. There were also other complications. My sisters and I went to visit him only once because of the distance and the severity of his condition. It was scary for me to see my strong father weak and in pain. He couldn't even talk because of the tracheotomy. I was so overwhelmed with emotion that I left without saying goodbye—something I regret to this day.

Days later we were told of his improvement and were encouraged that he would soon be home. He wrote us the letter that I included on this page. Things were looking better, but within a week we received the phone call. My mother called to tell my sisters and me that our father had died.

My heart still aches to think about him. I often wonder what it would be like to sit and talk with him as an adult. I wonder about the relationship we would have. One thing I know for sure, he would have had so much fun being a grandfather.

JEN MARTAKIS

★ Valparaiso, Indiana

As a mother of four beautiful children, my goal is to preserve the memories of our family for the future. I am fortunate that my wonderful husband, Nick, understands my love for scrapbooking. There is nothing like the satisfaction of creating a lasting journal of all the times of our lives.

LIFE CHANGING

SUPPLIES:
Textured cardstock (Bazzill); rub-on elements (My Mind's Eye); chipboard letters (Heidi Swapp); pen (American Crafts); distress ink (Ranger)

The Story Behind the Layout

"Breanne, did Tom Gonch die?" I first heard those words on Monday, January 31, around 10:30 in the morning, when my sister called my cell phone. I was scooping ice out of the ice machine at work. Those words have gone through my head over and over again throughout the last year. Unfortunately, my answer has changed from, "No, what are you talking about?" to "Yes." Tom passed away on Sunday, January 30, 2005. He was an amazing person—a person who loved everyone he met, a person that never said a mean word to anyone, a person who knew when someone needed a hug without words ever being spoken.

Losing a friend, especially when that friend is so young, is a numbing, life-changing experience. I had always considered myself blessed to have never had to face the death of a friend. After he passed away, my friends and I were overwhelmed with emotions and questions. We didn't understand how someone like Tom could be taken away at the age of eighteen, too young to live out his life to its full potential. Since he passed, my scrapbooking has become more real and I've put more of my feelings into my work. I think it's important for people to know that hurt and pain are real and should be addressed. I have found comfort through scrapbooking Tom's life and untimely death, and I have been able to relive my memories of him over and over again.

BREANNE CRAWFORD

★ *Scotch Plains, New Jersey*

Being "blessed" with a bad memory and a love for playing with paper and glue, my passion and love for scrapbooking has grown over the past eight years. Over the years, scrapbooking has become partners with my other addiction: shopping.

Although I wish that scrapbooking was my job, I play many other roles. I am a student in my third year at Seton Hall University studying social work. I work at a retail clothing store and work and teach classes at the local scrapbook store. I also baby-sit wonderful children, and intern at a social work agency.

When I'm not fulfilling one of those roles, I enjoy hanging out with friends, surfing the net, listening to music and, of course, scrapbooking. Scrapbooking is a journey to my innermost core, and I love that it helps me to explore myself.

easy peasy
mama

squeezy

MOMMY, iS YOUR SKIN OLD?

MOMMY, YOU are SO SOFT and SQUEEZY!

DO THE LINES on YOUR FACE HURT?

MOMMY, WHY DO YOU HAVE BOO BOO'S on YOUR FACE?

MOMMY, are YOU ALMOST a HUNDRED YEARS OLD?

LET'S PLAY HOUSE, YOU BE THE GRANDMA,

WHO NEEDS a CRUEL SELF-CONSCIENCE WHEN YOU HAVE TWO KIDS AGES 4 AND 6 THAT CAN BE SO BRUTALLY HONEST AT TIMES.

> "I MAY NOT HAVE GONE WHERE
> I INTENDED TO GO, BUT I THINK
> I HAVE ENDED UP WHERE
> I INTENDED TO BE."
> DOUGLAS NOEL ADAMS

LIFE GOES ON >>>

You wake up one morning and there you are…one day older, one day better. You realize that life doesn't stop, not even for a minute. You look back and wonder, "Have I done everything I wanted to do, did I see all of the things I wanted to see, or accomplish all of the things I wanted to accomplish? Am I where I wanted to be at this stage of my life? Have I made the most of each and every day?" If you haven't, what are you going to do about it? What do you think about when you ask yourself these questions? Do you think about your past, your mistakes and the experiences that have shaped you at this stage of your life? Or do you look toward the future?

We all get to a point in life where we ask ourselves these questions. Do you wonder what life would be like if things had been different? Or are you happy with the choices you made? Either way, life goes on.

EASY PEASY MAMA SQUEEZY

The Story Behind the Layout

SUPPLIES:
*Patterned papers (Provo Craft);
textured cardstock (Bazzill); letter
stickers (American Crafts); photo
corners (Heidi Swapp)*

Kids can be so brutally honest at times when it comes to sensitive subjects like age and weight. And although I am still young at heart, I can't help but take pause when they make comments about how old they think I am. I know they mean absolutely no harm or ill will; they are children and they speak their minds with honesty and good intentions. Now if they would just lay off the age jokes.

The title for the layout came from my six-year-old son. He is in kindergarten and, as any mom with a kindergartner can attest, that age is all about rhyming. What started as a one-liner on a *SpongeBobSquarePants* episode as "Easy Peasy Lemon Squeezy," wound up as "Easy Peasy Mama Squeezy." If it hadn't been for my shrill reaction, it would have been a "one-hit-wonder" one-liner. But with my gasp of a reaction, it was an instant giveaway that this saying could be used against me. At first, I insisted they never repeat the phrase again, but now I chuckle inside when they say it. I'm not trying to egg on the phrase, but it actually sounds young and hip when said aloud.

MONICA SCHOENEMANN

★ *Flower Mound, Texas*

Where should the hands point when it is:

MIDLIFE CRISIS?

YEAH, THAT'S RIGHT.

I GOT ONE AND I HAVE NO REGRETS!

...have always wanted a tattoo, but have been too chicken... ...detest needles.

...So, on a whim, my girlfriends and I went. After some drinks at a nearby bar, I did it. And it still hurt like hell.

Was it a mid-life crisis thing? Probably, but I have no regrets! I love my tattoo. There is something about it that makes me feel sexy, even half way through life.

TATTOO

SUPPLIES:
Patterned papers (7gypsies, Carolee's Creations, K&Company); twill (Stampington & Co.); ribbon (me & my BIG Ideas); photo turns (7gypsies); mini brads (All My Memories); paper flowers (Prima)

The Story Behind the Layout

I was at a BBQ and my girlfriends and I were talking about things we have always wanted to do. I have always wanted a tattoo, but I am terrified of needles. Both of my girlfriends already have tattoos, so on whim I said, "Let's go get one!" They promised me that "it didn't hurt." We went to the bar next door and downed a few shots—and then they made me go first. Don't let anyone tell you that a tattoo doesn't hurt. Even after drinks, it hurt like hell! I literally nearly fainted. But after it was all said and done, I love my tattoo! And it's true what they say—once you have one, you want another one. It's like childbirth: You forget the pain because the reward is worth it.

JOURNALING

I have always wanted a tattoo, but have been too chicken. I detest needles. So, on a whim, my girlfriends and I went. After some drinks at a nearby bar, I did it. And it hurt like hell. Was it a mid-life crisis thing? Probably, but I have no regrets! I love my tattoo. There is something about it that makes me feel sexy, even half way through life.

MIDLIFE CRISIS?

CHERYL LAU

★ Las Vegas, Nevada

I am a photographer and mixed-media artist, a wife to a wonderful husband and a mother of two, who became addicted to scrapbooking in September of 2005. My passions are adventure, exploring, learning, meeting people and being covered in glue and paint.

sound check

27

Test Test 1 2 3... Is this life on? 27 years 354 days old and I feel as the days tick by without much notice to me. Next tick of the clock and what? What dreams do I have? What do I look forward to? Is this age? Is this life? It's good, I am blessed but really I need a sound check a wake up call! Make a goal strive for more. Open my mouth and make a sound even if it needs adjustment at least it's the start of concert life!

SOUND CHECK

SUPPLIES:
Textured cardstock (Bazzill); acrylic
letters (Heidi Swapp); watercolor paints
(Chartpak); acrylic paint; stamping
ink; pen

JOURNALING

Test, test, 1, 2, 3...Is this life
on? 27 years, 304 days old
and I feel as the days tick
by without much notice to me.
Next tick of the clock and
what? What dreams do I have?
What do I look forward to?
Is this age? Is this life?
It's good, I am blessed, but
really I need a sound check,
a wake up call! Make a goal,
strive for more. Open my mouth
and make a sound. Even if it
needs adjustment, at least it's
the start of concert life!

The Story Behind the Layout

I have come to truly love creating pages that explore not only the mediums
of scrapbooking, but of all art forms. My trusty six-dollar watercolor kit has
brought so much life to my pages and "Soundcheck" is just another addition to
the collection of pages I've washed with watercolor. I created this page to help
me express my thoughts on my life as it is right now. I am content and happy,
but feel there is so much more in store for me. I need to make some noise,
make a mark on this world, no matter how small. I love keeping it real in all
my scrapbook pages. Even in my children's albums, between the obligatory
birthday and Christmas layouts, are pages full of depth and meaning...pages
that my children will read and learn from. In the future, when my children
happen upon this page, I want them to see that I am real, that I felt this way
even with all the love I have for them. I am an individual who has a need for
more than just being a caregiver...and that's OK. Someday they may feel the
same way. Knowing I felt it too will hopefully be comforting to them. That is
why I scrapbook to document our lives, for better or worse.

COURTNEY DELAURA

★ Medford, Oregon

I reside in Southern Oregon with
my two beautiful children, my
understanding husband and joyful
black Lab. I've been scrapbooking
since junior high, though those
albums were full of tape and Lisa
Frank stickers! I love the reminder
of how far I have come in capturing
the memories of my life. When I am not scrapbooking, I love to play golf in a
local women's league, chat with my two greatest friends, Heather Thompson
and Gina Lovato, paint and teach all things paper art at my local scrapbook
store, No Bare Pages Scrapbook Company. I have found my true passion in
combining photos, heartfelt journaling, paint and paper to create albums
that represent my true self. I thrive on keeping it real in life and art.

VAGUE

SUPPLIES:
Cardstock (Bazzill); rub-ons (FoofaLa, 7 gypsies); number stickers (Paperfever); ribbon (Scrapworks); brads (Queen & Co.); pen; marker; ink; thread

The Story Behind the Layout

My poor memory and concentration span are both a joke and a bit of a concern. Conversations will often go in one ear and out the other. I write myself notes to remember things and then forget where I left the notes. I have been known to share a story with friends, and when asked about it years later, I have no idea what they are talking about. To those who don't know me, I appear to have made the whole thing up! I think I need a better filing system for my cluttered brain.

I had been listening to this song by The Waifs, an Australian band, for a long time, thinking about how the lyrics could have been written for me. Eventually, I remembered to get around to making a layout about it. The convoluted stitching and journaling, and overgrown hand cut vines represent what it might feel like to be inside my head!

LORETTA GRAYSON

★ Emu Vale, Queensland, Australia

I live with my husband and three children in an old messy farmhouse in a beautiful part of Australia.

From an early age, I loved creating with paper and dreamed of becoming an artist. I still dream of making a living from my art, but in the meantime, I have had a number of sensible jobs, including being a primary school teacher, library assistant and volunteer counselor.

I have ideas in my head for magnificent artworks, which I have been procrastinating on the last twenty years or so. I do this by taking up one crafty hobby after another. I have a cupboard full of unfinished projects, and when I started scrapbooking, I fully expected it to go the same way.

I am overwhelmed by how much I have gained through the art of scrapbooking. I love that I can tell my family's story through these little artworks, and I have recently been exploring different ways of telling my own story. Scrapbooking has given me an outlet that allows me to feel creative again.

I KNOW I'M NOT IMMORTAL

SUPPLIES:

Patterned papers (Junkitz); textured cardstock (Bazzill); ribbon (Offray); rub-on letters (Making Memories, Scrapworks); chipboard letters (handmade); clear glaze (Ranger); colored staples (Making Memories); label maker (DYMO); acrylic paint; pen; twill tapes; vellum; cardstock

JOURNALING

Growing old—aging gracefully—I know it's a privilege—and I AM trying. But when the heck did this HAPPEN? One minute I'm young, and feeling invincible. Now, staring back at me in the mirror is a woman who, for the sake of vanity alone, is self-conscious about close-up photos. I tell myself, "those aren't wrinkles—those are souvenirs of your survival." But to everyone else, they're WRINKLES, plain and simple!

I've got all those little daily reminders that I'm not 20-, or even 30-something, anymore—those little daily pills that most of us will take when we get to "that age." I'm very thankful we have these medical marvels—but I still wish I didn't need them yet!

Yes, I'm a survivor, and I know it. I've survived multiple surgeries & illnesses, including cancer. I've experienced losses of people I love, failures and disappointments. Through them all, I've become stronger in spirit and wiser in perspective. It's the VANITY that makes me want to LOOK 20- or even 30-something, with the wisdom and experiences of my true age. I know, with a lot of money and a good doctor, I could make that happen, but the practical side of me says "Oh no, you don't!"

So how about just a FEW LESS daily reminders of this aging thing—think you could arrange that, God?

The Story Behind the Layout

Picture three over-forty women sitting around chatting about everything and nothing...of course, the subject of the trials and tribulations of getting "older" would come into the conversation soon or later! Three "mature" women talking and giggling over the aching muscles in places that never ached before...the need for more sleep than we remember needing before...the pills we line up with our orange juice and most necessary cup of coffee every morning...and let's not forget the chemical help we need now to keep our hair color the same as when we were younger! This is the conversation that inspired me to make a layout about how I truly feel after realizing that I'm not thirty-something anymore, and no longer immune to the inevitable effects of aging, and how grateful I am that I'm still here to light-heartedly "complain" about it!

KATHY MONTGOMERY

★ Rocklin, California

My husband Erik and I live north of Sacramento with our overactive springer spaniel Kylie. I spent the first twenty-seven years of my professional life in the business community, most recently as a human resources manager, but in the summer of 2000, after moving (planned) and becoming seriously ill (totally unplanned) at the same time, I wanted to make some major changes to my lifestyle. Thanks to the support of my husband, I was able to do just that. I've been a crafter for as long as I can remember, going back to my childhood, and began "safe" scrapbooking in that summer of 2000. Now I'm not only enjoying my scrapbooking as a personal hobby, but I do freelance design work for a scrapbooking manufacturer, an online scrapbooking site, and work part-time at my local scrapbook store. My life is still hectic, and sometimes tiring, but I'm sure having fun now!

Needless to say, I don't have a *house staff* to do the 10+ loads of laundry a week, nor a *chef* to prepare well balanced, low-fat meals, nor a *chauffeur* to transport two children to and from their daily afternoon/weekend activities. No, like many other corporate, **MID**dle-class women, I wear those hats plus some. Now, as I embark on a new stage of my **LIFE**, I find things seem to be *WAY* more hectic for me now then ever before. I'm constantly trying to squeeze out another hour or two from somewhere in my day. Do I stress over things? *Sure,* I do! Some days worry steals my strength causing near **CRISIS** level meltdown. Most days I meet *it head on!* I'm a master juggler, juggling conflicts and responsibilities, choosing the battles that need fighting, and thankfully tapping into my "girlfriend" network when I'm in need of an infusion of sanity. I'm **FOR**tunate enough to come from an awesome stock of "*strong*" women who dealt with a multitude of challenging circumstances in their day. Quitting wasn't an option. They struggled, managed and persevered. So, even though I'd like more "**ME**" time to maintain an agreeable attitude, no way would I contemplate shaming my heritage by "*falling apart*." I'm far too proud. Besides, there are more important things to manage, such as raising healthy, self-assured children, as well as providing support to my "*road-warrior*" husband. As I stated in the beginning, I don't have time to undergo a mid-life crisis that I so richly deserve, but more importantly, I don't want to!

I have -**NO**- time to have the "mid-life" crisis that I <u>deserve</u>. OK, so my life choices didn't put me on the treadmill for wealth and riches.

No Mid-Life Crisis 4 me

ART
AWESOME
vivid
ATTITUDE

i

NO MID-LIFE CRISIS 4 ME

SUPPLIES:
Patterned papers (KI Memories, My Mind's Eye, Provo Craft); acrylic flowers (Heidi Swapp); ribbon, brads, photo corner (Making Memories); colored dots (KI Memories); birthday border (Provo Craft); chipboard words (Li'l Davis Designs); chipboard letters (Pressed Petals); fiber (BasicGrey)

The Story Behind the Layout

I'm always creating layouts about my children because that is usually where my mind rests. However, I know it will be important to them to have some insight about their mother, and how she views herself. In coming up with describing an important stage in my life, I immediately focused on my present-day experiences. It's important that my kids know every stage in one's life can be challenging, yet should never be viewed as crippling. This is my third quarter "crunch" time. I'm hustling and maneuvering my life choices to ensure that my children have brighter futures. As the caretaker of my children's early and adolescent years, I'm entrusted to love and teach them ways that prepare them for their own demanding life stages. More often than not, you teach through examples as my forbearers did. My message to them in this layout is prepare yourself to make good choices, prepare yourself to accept the consequences of bad choices, work smart and never give up. These are my guiding forces that lift me up through those taxing life stages.

JILL
JACKSON-MILLS

★ Roswell, Georgia

I am married to a gentle giant from Tennessee and living in metro Atlanta for the past fourteen years. I am a corporate mom with two very active children, Drew and Alex, and a wonderful purebred Akita named Chai. Photography has always been a big passion of mine, but scrapbooking adds just the right spice and flavor to ignite that passion into a mild obsession. I consider myself an eclectic artist. I don't limit myself to just one certain style. I enjoy dabbling in a variety of techniques and styles. I am inspired by a multitude of things, but especially if it's charged in color, spirit or design.

RESOURCES

The following companies manufacture products featured in this book. Please check your local retailers to find these materials, or go to a company's Web site for the latest product. In addition, we have made every attempt to properly credit the items mentioned in this book. We apologize to any company that we have listed incorrectly, and we would appreciate hearing from you.

7 Gypsies
(877) 749-7797
www.sevengypsies.com

All My Memories
(888) 553-1998
www.allmymemories.com

American Crafts
(801) 226-0747
www.americancrafts.com

American Tag Company
(800) 223-3956
www.americantag.net

Amscan, Inc.
(800) 444-8887
www.amscan.com

Anna Griffin, Inc.
(888) 817-8170
www.annagriffin.com

Art Institute Glitter, Inc.
(928) 639-0805
www.artglitter.com

Autumn Leaves
(800) 588-6707
www.autumnleaves.com

Basic Grey™
(801) 451-6006
www.basicgrey.com

Bazzill Basics Paper
(480) 558-8557
www.bazzillbasics.com

Berwick Offray™, LLC
(800) 344-5533
www.offray.com

Bobarbo
(418) 748-6775
www.bobarbo.com

Bo-Bunny Press
(801) 771-4010
www.bobunny.com

Camden Fair - no contact info

Captured Elements, LLC
(816) 985-9129
www.capturedelements.com

Carolee's Creations®
(435) 563-1100
www.ccpaper.com

ChartPak
(800) 628-1910
www.chartpak.com

Chatterbox, Inc.
(208) 939-9133
www.chatterboxinc.com

Clearsnap, Inc.
(360) 293-6634
www.clearsnap.com

Creative Imaginations
(800) 942-6487
www.cigift.com

Daisy D's Paper Company
(888) 601-8955
www.daisydspaper.com

Darice, Inc.
(800) 321-1494
www.darice.com

DecoArt™ Inc.
(800) 367-3047
www.decoart.com

Dèjá Views
(800) 243-8419
www.dejaviews.com

Deluxe Designs
(480) 497-9005
www.deluxedesigns.com

Die Cuts With A View
(801) 224-6766
www.diecutswithaview.com

DMD Industries, Inc.
(800) 805-9890
www.dmdind.com

Doodlebug Design™ Inc.
(801) 966-9952
www.doodlebug.ws

Dymo
(800) 426-7827
www.dymo.com

EK Success™, Ltd.
(800) 524-1349
www.eksuccess.com

Everlasting Keepsakes™ by faith
(816) 896-7037
www.everlastinkeepsakes.com

Fiskars®, Inc.
(800) 950-0203
www.fiskars.com

Flair® Designs
(888) 546-9990
www.flairdesignsinc.com

Flaming Pear
www.flamingpear.com

FontWerks
(604) 942-3105
www.fontwerks.com

Fredrix Artist Canvas
www.fredrixartistcanvas.com

Georgia-Pacific Corporation
(404) 652-4000
www.gp.com

Heidi Swapp/Advantus Corporation
(904) 482-0092
www.heidiswapp.com

Hero Arts® Rubber Stamps, Inc.
(800) 822-4376
www.heroarts.com

Imagination Project, Inc.
(513) 860-2711
www.imaginationproject.com

Jeneva & Company
(541) 928-6925
www.jenevaandcompany.com

Jest Charming
(702) 564-5101
www.jestcharming.com

Junkitz™
(732) 792-1108
www.junkitz.com

K & Company
(888) 244-2083
www.kandcompany.com

Karen Foster Design
(801) 451-9779
www.karenfosterdesign.com

Keeping Memories Alive™
(800) 419-4949
www.scrapbooks.com

Ken Brown Stamps/Rubber Stamps of
America
(800) 553-5031
www.stampusa.com

KI Memories
(972) 243-5595
www.kimemories.com

Krylon®
(216) 566-200
www.krylon.com

Leaving Prints™
(801) 426-0636
www.leavingprints.com

Letraset - no contact info

Li'l Davis Designs
(949) 838-0344
www.lildavisdesigns.com

Magic Mesh
(651) 345-6374
www.magicmesh.com

Magic Scraps™
(972) 238-1838
www.magicscraps.com

Making Memories
(800) 286-5263
www.makingmemories.com

Mara-Mi, Inc.
(800) 627-2648
www.mara-mi.com

Marvy® Uchida/ Uchida of America, Corp.
(800) 541-5877
www.uchida.com

Maya Road, LLC
(214) 488-3279
www.mayaroad.com

May Arts
(800) 442-3950
www.mayarts.com

me & my BiG ideas®
(949) 883-2065
www.meandmybigideas.com

Michaels® Arts & Crafts
(800) 642-4235
www.michaels.com

Morex Corporation
(717) 852-7771
www.morexcorp.com

My Mind's Eye™, Inc.
(800) 665-5116
www.frame-ups.com

Offray- see Berwick Offray, LLC

Paper Adventures®
(973) 406-5000
www.paperadventures.com

Paper Company, The/ANW Crestwood
(800) 525-3196
www.anwcrestwood.com

Paper Fever, Inc.
(800) 477-0902
www.paperfever.com

Paper Loft
(866) 254-1961
www.paperloft.com

Pebbles Inc.
(801) 224-1857
www.pebblesinc.com

Pentel of America, Ltd.
(800) 421-1419
www.pentel.com

Plaid Enterprises, Inc.
(800) 842-4197
www.plaidonline.com

Polar Bear Press
(801) 451-7670
www.polarbearpress.com

Pressed Petals
(800) 748-4656
www.pressedpetals.com

Prima Marketing, Inc.
(909) 627-5532
www.mulberrypaperflowers.com

Prism™ Papers
(866) 902-1002
www.prismpapers.com

Provo Craft®
(888) 577-3545
www.provocraft.com

PSX Design™
(800) 782-6748
www.psxdesign.com

Purple Onion Designs
www.purpleoniondesigns.com

Queen & Co.
(858) 485-5132
www.queenandcompany.com

Ranger Industries, Inc.
(800) 244-2211
www.rangerink.com

Rusty Pickle
(801) 746-1045
www.rustypickle.com

Sakura of America
(800) 776-6257
www.sakuraofamerica.com

Sanford® Corporation
(800) 323-0749
www.sanfordcorp.com

Scenic Route Paper Co.
(801) 785-0761
www.scenicroutepaper.com

The ScrapRoom
(888) 820-9513
www.scrap-room.com

Scrapworks, LLC
(801) 363-1010
www.scrapworks.com

SEI, Inc.
(800) 333-3279
www.shopsei.com

Sizzix®
(866) 742-4447
www.sizzix.com

Stamp Craft- see Plaid Enterprises

Stampin' Up!®
(800) 782-6787
www.stampinup.com

Stampington & Company
(877) STAMPER
www.stampington.com

Staples, Inc.
(800) 3STAPLE
www.staples.com

Sticker Studio™
(208) 322-2465
www.stickerstudio.com

Technique Tuesday, LLC
(503) 644-4073
www.techniquetuesday.com

Tsukineko®, Inc.
(800) 769-6633
www.tsukineko.com

Urban Lily- no contact info

Wal-Mart Stores, Inc.
(800) WALMART
www.walmart.com

We R Memory Keepers, Inc.
(801) 539-5000
www.weronthenet.com

Wordsworth
(719) 282-3495
www.wordsworthstamps.com

INDEX OF ARTISTS

INDEX OF TOPICS

EXPRESS YOURSELF
WITH THESE OTHER TITLES FROM
MEMORY MAKERS AND NORTH LIGHT BOOKS!

Collage Discovery Workshop:
Beyond the Unexpected

ISBN-10: 1-58180-678-7
ISBN-13: 978-1-58180-678-6
paperback, 128 pages, 33267

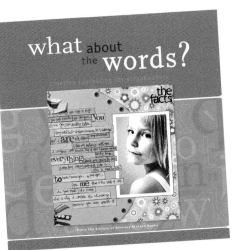

What About the Words

ISBN-10: 1-892127-77-6
ISBN-13: 978-1-892127-77-8
paperback, 128 pages, Z0017

Your Scrapbook Your Story

ISBN-10: 1-892127-60-1
ISBN-13: 978-1-892127-60-0
paperback, 128 pages, 33437

THESE BOOKS AND OTHERS BY F+W PUBLICATIONS, INC. ARE AVAILABLE FROM YOUR LOCAL ART OR CRAFT RETAILER, BOOKSTORE OR ONLINE SUPPLIER.